POLITICS
AND
UNIVERSAL ETHICS

Shimon Cowen

Connor Court Publishing
Ballarat, Australia

Published in 2011 by Connor Court Publishing Pty Ltd.

Connor Court Publishing Pty Ltd.

PO Box 224W

Ballarat VIC 3350

sales@connorcourt.com

www.connorcourt.com

National Library of Australia Cataloguing-in-Publication entry

Cowen, Shimon Dovid.

Title: Politics and universal ethics / Shimon Cowen.

ISBN: 9781921421815 (pbk.)

Subjects: Religion and ethics.

Ten commandments--Criticism, interpretation, etc.

Islamic ethics.

Christian ethics.

Jewish ethics.

Religion and politics.

Dewey Number: 291.5

Front cover pricture: "Hula Valley from Ramot Naftali" (detail) by Victor Majzner, used with permission.

CONTENTS

ACKNOWLEDGEMENTS

My first debt of gratitude is to my wife Miriam, who not only reviewed the manuscript, but has also weathered the vicissitudes of the Institute for Judaism and Civilization, that has enabled me to dedicate myself to the research, projects and involvements which produced these writings. Dr Mat Gelman also offered helpful comments on the manuscript. I am grateful next to many colleagues, men and women of faith and politics, who have joined me in forums and actions, which shared the goal of a convergence of law and morality, of politics and a higher conscience. I am grateful also to the supporters of the Institute for Judaism and Civilization and Jewish Education Association of Victoria, without whose generosity these writings would not have seen the light of day. Finally thanks are due to Dr Anthony Cappello of Connor Court Publishing for his support of this project.

The first chapter "The adversary culture" appeared in *Quadrant* in October 2009 as "'Rights' as a weapon in culture war". The second chapter was first published in the *Journal of Judaism and Civilization*, Vol 8, 2009, as "Letters to Parliament". The third chapter "'Right' and 'left' in universal ethics" has been pre-published as a contribution to the *Journal of Judaism and Civilization*, Vol 9, 2011. The fourth chapter is a reworked version of the essay "Eternal law and human legislation" which appeared in the *Journal of Judaism and Civilization*, Vol 1, 1998. The fifth chapter includes several essays printed in *Interface*, the newsletter of the Institute for Judaism and Civilization over 2009-2010. All of the above are reproduced by kind permission and have undergone further editing.

Rabbi Dr Shimon Cowen,
Director, Institute for Judaism and Civilization,
Adjunct Research Associate in the School of Philosophical, Historical and International Studies, Monash University

INTRODUCTION

This book is the product of a "universal reflection" in a specific political context. The context is Australia, and within Australia, primarily the State of Victoria. I am confident that this will have relevance elsewhere, for it is about contemporary western society, reflected in one of its provinces. What has happened here has either happened elsewhere already or is elsewhere on the political agenda – with more to come.

The "universality" of the reflection has to do with what I term an objective universal ethics. According to universal ethics, there is right and there is wrong, and right is basically always right and wrong is basically always wrong ("objectively") – under all times and circumstances ("universally"). The standard was set by the Creator at Mount Sinai more than 3000 years ago in a revelation, of which the Ten Commandments form the core, and before that in the teachings which the Creator made known to Abraham, the father of the great world religions and cultures.[1]

The moral covenant between humanity and its Creator consists of a number of basic laws with many details, known as the laws of Noah or the Noahide laws after the Biblical survivor of the Flood and father of humanity, Noah. The tradition of these ethical laws,

---

1 These include not only Judaism, Christianity and Islam but also Hinduism in accordance with tradition which explains that when Abraham sent his sons to the "East", they there propagated certain key teachings, which found their way into Hinduism. See footnote 86.

the root morality of the world religions which surfaces in and out of human consciousness throughout history, has most recently been endorsed by leaders of two great continents. In 1991 the American President, George Herbert Walker Bush, together with Congress endorsed them, in a preamble to a Bill establishing Education Day, as "the bedrock of society since the dawn of civilization".[2] In 2008, the Governor General of Australia, Michael Jeffery issued a statement that the "Seven Noahide laws...or ethical principles apply to all contemporary issues".[3] Some have referred to this tradition as a "Judeo-Christian" tradition, but in fact it is both wider and more specific. This tradition can find resonance, beyond Judaism and Christianity, in adherents of Islam, as well as in some aspects of the Eastern religions. At the same time, the substance of this tradition is specific. It is a tradition of specific moral and ethical laws.

This book is not about the specific content of these laws, though their application to some contemporary issues will be clear in the course of its discussion. I have written on the world view of the Noahide laws in my monograph *Perspectives on the Noahide laws,* and have published studies in the actual ethical detail of the laws in issues of the *Bulletin in Noahide law.* This, present book is about what is involved in bringing these laws and moral standards into political practice.

In this book several writings, written over a number of years, are thematically assembled. Because they were written at different times as stand-alone pieces, they do not form a perfectly seamless continuity. There are some overlaps, and differences of tense, in their discussions. Nevertheless, they do form a sequence and structure, in which each makes a distinct point (or set of related points).

The structure of the book is in three parts. Part 1 addresses the contemporary "challenge to universal ethics". The first chapter deals with the culture and philosophy of this challenge. The second chapter shows this culture at work in the legislative year of the

2 Public Law 102-14, 102nd Congress, First Session, H.J. Res 104.
3 Quoted in the Institute (for Judaism and Civilization) Review, October 2008

Victorian Parliament in 2008. It contains a number of critiques of bills, which were subjected to intense struggle and yet succeeded in being passed in that year.

The second part, "Questions for a politics of universal ethics", deals in a more theoretical vein with important questions which can be asked about the "human face" of a universal ethics. Chapters 3 and 4 address the questions of how a Divinely sanctioned ethics makes room for a natural human-political diversity of temperament, and how it goes together with a role for human sensitivity and "autonomy" in legislation. These chapters are more abstract in character. They move between analysis of the historical tradition of universal ethics from Sinai and the western political and legal tradition, into which universal ethics are to be transposed. Some seeking a "lighter" read could initially skip these two chapters, and return to them later for completeness and rigour in understanding the political practice and "installation" of universal ethics.

The third and final part of the book "Towards a politics of universal ethics" examines, as its sole Chapter (5) indicates, "Entry points to a politics of universal ethics". It is assembled also out of a number of short essays written in a mode of proposal and exploration for ways and conditions under which universal ethics could become the parameter and moral perimeter of contemporary politics.

As mentioned, the impetus for the writing of the first two chapters of this book came in the year 2008 when a fundamental legislative transformation was attempted and achieved in the Victorian Parliament. Its issues have since spread to other State legislatures in Australia. A new round of struggle is about to open this year (2011) at the Federal level. The Federal Parliament of Australia faces two major debates, one on voluntary euthanasia and another on homosexual marriage. In terms of the spiritual tradition of universal ethics these have to do with the overturning of fundamental anchor prohibitions of society. In this case, these are the prohibition on killing and on forbidden sexual unions, in which homosexual practice, along with incest, adultery and bestiality are included.

The tradition of universal ethics is consciously termed a *spiritual* tradition. As its name indicates, it has to do with something *more* than reason. Its function is not to displace or dispense with reason, but to tutor reason. The role of universal ethics is to establish the first principles, the contours and principles of reason, which reason itself cannot supply, but necessarily takes from somewhere else. What will persuade us to accept the first principles supplied by the ethical tradition from Sinai is accordingly not reason, since, as stated, reason does not produce first principles. These first principles will be recognized and ratified only by the human soul itself. For the soul, "made in the image of G-d", natively resonates with ethical principles, which are G-d-given and which embody Divine attributes.

This is also a basis for the claim to universality of these ethics. Everyone has a soul, however unconscious or repressed. It needs only to be evoked through some act of self transcendence to test and demonstrate its resonance with these universal values.

Spiritually disconnected "reason" could justify both voluntary and active euthanasia (including "assisted suicide") as well as homosexual practice. But it can do so only by importing value judgments and making intellectual moves, which the Divine text and template explicitly anticipates and negates.

A tradition of commentary, which starts from Sinai, addresses the Biblical verse prohibiting suicide.

> However [if you shed] your blood – of your souls – I shall require [an expiation]...[4]

This follows another verse, which permitted humanity, after the Flood, to kill animals in order to eat them. Until then humanity had been permitted to use animals for work, but not to kill them

---

4 Genesis 9:5.

in order to eat their flesh. Why does the prohibition of suicide immediately follow the biblical permission to slaughter animals in order to eat their flesh? The answer given[5] is that in the previous verse we learnt that animals, which had been previously placed in the service of humanity for work and other benefits, may now be killed for food. So too, one might think, one's own body is also within one's own jurisdiction. *Consequently*, just as one is permitted to kill the animals in one's jurisdiction for personal benefit, so might one kill the body within one's jurisdiction for one's own personal benefit (to escape pain and suffering). To forestall this consequence, the verse teaches that one may not commit suicide. The reason is stated in a subsequent verse "...for in the image of G-d, He [G-d] made the human".[6] The human being has a soul made in the image of G-d and the body, which houses that soul, may not be destroyed by suicide. A person does not have jurisdiction over his or her body to treat it in this way.

With regard to homosexuality and homosexual impulse, the biblical text states:

> Therefore a man shall leave his father and mother and cleave to his wife, and they shall become one flesh.[7]

This "cleaving", which refers also to a sexual union, is imaginable between two men and between a human and animal, but both of these have been prohibited by the biblical text. It permits only the cleaving of a man and woman. Their union has the possibility of producing, and their union is expressed in, "one flesh", namely the child born of their union. It does not deny that a human being might have a strong desire, or even tendency, for one of these forbidden sexual unions. Yet it forestalls the reasoning – with whatever imported assumptions or claimed "first principles" – which would move to permit it.

---

5 See the commentary of *Rashi* on Genesis 9:5 and the super-commentary of *B'er BaSodeh* on *Rashi* there.
6 Genesis 9:6.
7 Genesis 2:24.

The tradition of universal ethics is not indifferent to human pain, suffering and passion. Indeed this tradition taught the world charity and regard for others. The higher moral template properly arbitrates our response to pain, suffering and passion. It gave reason, feeling and action their human and civilized form, their first principles and moral methodology. The orientation to a G-d-given universal ethics does not make the human being an automaton. It makes the human being aware of his or her own spiritual identity as made in the image of G-d, with its normative map. This strengthens and frees a person to the task of carrying out a Divine moral agency, which brings with it self-actualisation, autonomy and creativity. This agency is, via an ethical human practice, to make the world into a residence for the manifestation of the Divine. Peace, happiness, goodness and human self-transcendence all coalesce in this purpose and goal.

PART 1:
THE POLITICAL CHALLENGE
TO UNIVERSAL ETHICS

1
THE ADVERSARY CULTURE

The legislative season of the Victorian Parliament in 2008 introduced profound changes to basic social institutions and norms, and opened up a fundamental conflict of values, in our society – and in the Parliament itself. It has conjured the spectre of a "cultural struggle" between two sets of values. One set of values is anchored in the common tradition of the world religions and holds to objective, universal and enduring values, representing the moral covenant of the Creator and the conscience or soul of the human being. The second is rooted in an essentially materialistic and secularist philosophy (whether consciously embraced by its supporters or not), which prevailed and spawned the legislative changes. We are at a crossroads now and it is not only a virtue, but also a necessity, to examine the fundamental choice of first principles, which is at issue in our society and globally.

Democracy and values

In better times the idea of a bill of rights might have been greeted with pleasure by those who want to protect freedom of religion. Now it is rightly viewed with suspicion and apprehension since it occurs in the midst of a cultural struggle, which is opening up in our society and could be used as an instrument against religion in that struggle. The issues are becoming clearer. The greyness, which results from a mixture of white and black, is sometimes welcomed as an expression of the complexity and subtlety of issues ("not everything is black or white"). At the same time greyness, like twilight for a motorist, can be dangerous. So too in a moral greyness, there is no contrast, the issues are not clear and judgment faces self-deception.

We live in a time in which a State Government in Victoria in one legislative year, legislated abortion on demand[8], potentially licensing the unlimited destruction of unborn babies every year, without any questions asked; reengineered the laws of de facto unions so as to create a functional equivalent of homosexual marriage (in all but name) in a "Relationships Bill"; and by IVF legislation established the notion of "commissioning" biologically parentless children. There are those who fought for these things – amongst them the "high media", academia and the appointed bureaucratic commissions – and there are those who see them as moral ills. The result of the implementation of these changes is a great rupture with thousands of years of shared human values. Great masses of people look on, not really knowing what to think or what to teach their children.

The sides to the conflict appear to be, and indeed are, "religious" and "secular". Yet those, who wanted and achieved these changes, invoked principles which purported to have to do with democracy. Two areas of democratic theory which were invoked in this regard are (a) "the separation of religion and state" and (b) "human rights". In fact, as we shall argue, the issue has nothing to do with either of these. They only obscure a conflict, which is essentially about values and the principles which form the source of those values.

The separation of religion and state

With regard to the separation of religion and state, as this doctrine is expressed in both the American and Australian constitutions, the provision is that the State shall not *establish* a particular religion. Prima

---

8 For foetuses up to 24 weeks, without any questions being asked and up to birth if two opinions could be cited to support it.

facie, this posed no conflict with affirmations in both societies of a neutral monotheism. The Preamble to the Australian Constitution speaks of its constituents "humbly relying on the blessing of Almighty G-d", and the American Declaration of Independence speaks of "nature's laws and nature's G-d" and indeed the American currency bears the motto "In G-d we trust". The fact is that both of these societies were, and in the overwhelming majority still are, religiously identifying and believing societies. The statements of these prefatory documents expressed a grass-roots fact: belief in G-d was and is the default *empirical* position of both societies.

The principle stated in section 116 of the Australian Constitution and in the First Amendment to the American Constitution does not require that religion be purged from the public square. The simple import of the separation of Religion and State is that religion shall not be prescribed (or curtailed) by the State. The State, enjoying the exclusive legitimate power to exercise force, whether internally through the police or externally through its military forces, is an administrative entity. Religion is different: it is a source of values. The State *per se* cannot prescribe religion, but religion, just like other values, may well up within the body politic – the public – to influence the policies of the state.

The idea that state institutions – parliamentary, educational or other – must not in their legislation, policy or other content *express* religion or religious values or view has nothing to with the separation of religion and State. It is a covert ideology of secularism, which proscribes the embodiment in public policy of ethical values based on the authority of religious teaching. Secularism of this kind is an ideology which, paradoxically, seeks the absolute unity of the state with religion – its own "religion" of atheistic materialism. According to the intent of the Australian and American constitutions, state policy and state institutions must allow currents of values, including religiously inspired values, to proceed from the public square, and give them representative significance. The *a priori* exclusion of religiously inspired values from public institutions is, in this constitutional setting, an ideological coup against religion.

The attempt to exclude religious values from public institutions by an ideological secularism operates on both theoretical and practical planes. There is first of all the theoretical construct, set out by writers such as Amy Gutmann[9], of a shared "public reason": a religious discourse, it is argued, cannot be admitted to the discussion of public policy, because it does not represent accepted shared values. The fact that personal religious identification is acknowledged by 70 per cent of the Australian and more of the American public – i.e. that religious identification is the salient fact of the "public" – is overlooked.

The practical aspect of the attempt on "democratic" grounds to create a religiously neutralized public, is to argue that wherever public funding is concerned, religious institutions or providers must yield to purported "neutral public" standards. This reasoning, as we shall note below could well impact on religious schools in Victoria. The problem with this reasoning is that these funds come from a public which overwhelmingly identifies with religious experience. The "public", in truth, is no more than a space in which values which are actually held, may enter into discussion and be given their representative weight.

Human rights

The second area of democratic theory, which is claimed as support by those who wished to introduce the changes, has to do with "human rights". The former Chief Justice of the High Court of Australia, Justice Murray Gleeson, has introduced here a vital caution, stated in

9 See for example Amy Gutmann, *Identity in Democracy*, Princeton: Princeton University Press, 2003.

the clearest simplicity, that purported rights are anchored in values.[10] A "right" is as good or as true as the value it represents. The only problem is that the language of "rights" insulates the claimed "right" from public discussion and consigns it to a judicial preserve, whilst that of "values", as a matter for public, moral discussion, does not. When rights become the subject of international law, they acquire an even greater mystique. We struggle to accommodate our positions to international Charters of rights. The difference is that international law, which is binding only by subscription (and then is weakly enforceable), bites less. But these too are no more than the statements of values, and are no truer or more binding than the values which underpin them.

The point could be highlighted by the question: "Is there a right to marry one's sibling?" The answer is simply a matter of held values. For one coming from the great religious traditions, the answer is obviously, no. For an atheistic and materialistic secularism, the answer might be, yes. The question has been tested in Sweden. In Sweden incest and marriage between half-siblings is legal. By definition incest has become a right. In Australia and in America it is illegal and therefore there is no such right.

The very term "rights", with its Enlightenment lineage, has to do with a concept of the autonomy and sovereignty of the human being. Religion, whilst acknowledging human free will, looks also at the Sovereignty of G-d and the role of human agency in the fulfilment of Divine purpose. The deficit in the Enlightenment version of rights is often corrected by adding to the word "rights"– "and obligations". There is after all, "freedom from" and "freedom to", negative and positive freedom. But *both posited rights and obligations*

---

10 "To describe something as a 'right' may itself require justification. It is a commonplace feature of political and legal debate that advocates of various interests seek to characterise those interests as rights, thereby staking a claim for weight or recognition that may be contestable. By calling an interest a right, you may trump another interest. If there is a contest, then, again, it can only be resolved rationally (as distinct from resolution by power or weight of numbers) by reference to some value." "Rights and values", speech delivered by Chief Justice Murray Gleeson to the Melbourne Catholic Lawyers Association on 18 June 2004.

are ultimately anchored in values, and it is the *values* which found them – not the arcane privilege and fundamental status conferred upon them by the term "rights" – which needs to be kept in the foreground of discussion.

What we do see, however, is that religious viewpoints in public policy are by no means intrinsically precluded by democratic concepts such the division of religion and state or by human rights under the Australian or American constitutions. On the other hand, a democratic society is capable of legitimating and installing (in the case of Sweden) values which for millennia have been considered contrary to civilization: incest. At issue is not democracy, but the values which will in fact prevail within the public and so find their way through to public policy.

The philosophy of contemporary secularism: "Hedonomat"

A new historical variant of materialism

To characterize the teaching of the dominant school of contemporary materialistic secularism, I have chosen the word "Hedonomat". It is a nickname for what I would in full term "Hedonistic Materialism". It contains a conscious allusion to the formulaic term "Diamat" – short for "Dialectical Materialism" – which was the official doctrine of the Eastern European and Russian communism, before it collapsed. The allusion has a hint of caricature, meaning to suggest that as squarely as "Diamat" dominated a vast empire, so also does the self-disciplined officialdom of "Hedonomat" seek to exert hegemony in Western liberal democratic societies. It is not backed by naked force, such as a secret (and not-so secret) police, as was Diamat in the Communist world. Rather it is achieved in the academic world, by a vast voluntary self-censorship or collective repression of the "personal experience of religious faith", described by the outgoing President of the British Royal Society of Psychiatrists, as the "unspeakable" taboo at the end of the twentieth century.[11] Its adherents substantially staff academia, major sections of the non-tabloid media, State television and radio and bureaucratic elites. In other words, it is found pre-eminently in the *non-grass-roots* culture of our society.

One of the ideological parents of Hedonomat is Darwin, from whose work a cosmology has been fashioned, a thoroughgoing materialism, which places the amoeba and the human being in a one-dimensional developmental spectrum. Under the Diamat of the Communist empire (in its classical Hegelian and Marxian terms), the driver of the human self-concept was essentially the concept of freedom and the overcoming of human self-alienation. The human self-concept in the materialism of Hedonomat, however, has a *hedonistic* driver, which comes from Freud and a revamped utilitarianism, the calculus of pleasure and pain. The Darwinism of Hedonomat places the human within nature; its Freudianism and utilitarianism aligns human self-realization with the interest of animals in the achievement of pleasure and freedom from pain.

The novelty of Hedonomat is thus that it looks at the fundamental characteristic of the human being as its animality, its instinctualism and its pleasure principle. Aside from abortion on demand, in public policy (as projected in its writings) this may mean killing only in order to escape pain or burden at either end of life: the "retarded" infant or the elderly incurably sick. Another hallmark of Hedonomat is the deregulation of sexual activity. This includes not only the normalization of homosexual practice, but in Peter Singer's writing, also the permission of bestiality[12] and in Swedish society, the legitimation of incest between half-siblings.

---

11 A . Sims, Presidential valedictory address to the (British) Royal College of Psychiatrists, published in the *British Journal of Psychiatry* (165) 1994, p. 445.
12 Peter Singer, "Heavy petting" published on nerve.com, 2001.

The atheism of Hedonomat

On a plain reading, the social cosmology developed out of Darwinism itself does not allow the concept of a qualitatively different human soul, about which the Bible writes. It does not acknowledge that the essential dimension of the human was fashioned in the image of G-d. By definition, Darwinism's materialistic developmentalism negates the concept of a Creator G-d. It removes the great G-d from the universe and the small G-d, the soul, from the human being. To preserve a concept of the human soul as constituting perhaps the major significance of the life of a human being, and its difference from the rest of creation, according to Hedonomat, is not only false but "species-ist". According to the Biblical account and traditional religion, on the other hand, the soul was given to the human being, and primacy given to the human being in creation, not for the sake of simple domination, but, to the contrary, so that the human being act as an agency of the Divine in the creation, transforming and elevating it and emancipating it. From the religious standpoint the human being is three-dimensional, possessed of a material body, a mind and a soul; and the soul is the ultimate informant and guide of body and mind.

The recognition of the transcendent Divine, and the values mandated by the transcendent Divine, is achieved essentially by the human soul, not by the human intellect. The soul non-cognitively experiences G-d. From the soul comes a humility, which allows the person to embrace the concept of a Divinity which transcends human intellect. The adage goes that "There are no atheists in the trenches", but the art is to recognize one's creatureliness and dependency outside the trenches, even when, materially, one is "riding high". Humility extends to the recognition that not only the human body, but also the human intellect is a created entity, and is therefore quite limited in its grasp of its Creator. Only the soul, a reflector of the Divine, can truly recognize and thereby "establish" the existence of an infinite Creator. For Hedonomat, the intellect is little more than an albeit scientifically sophisticated *guardian* of the animal within the human: such was the function of the "ego" for the "id" in Freudian theory. For Freud, intellect is there to organize, as rationally as possible, the maximization of pleasure and the minimization of pain. For Freud and Hedonomat, mind has the task of grasping and organizing the material world, not of submitting to the transcendental guidance of the soul.

Because the mind of Hedonomat cannot explain suffering, seemingly incompatible with the notion of a benevolent G-d, it therefore rejects G-d. The response of religion, that "My thoughts are not your thoughts nor are your ways my ways"[13] is beyond the Hedonomat practitioner. Hedonomat cannot or will not acknowledge that a transcendent logic and providence operates, which will eventually make evident G-d's goodness, notwithstanding and even through the bad of present suffering. This is because religion calls for self-transcendence, including transcendence of the limits of intellect. The biblical text (and millennia of religious tradition) is discredited by Hedonomat's summary attacks on passages of the Bible without informed understanding of these passages. Only a genuine exposure to theology and the tradition of commentary on these passages can make them properly understood.

Hedonomat and the morphing across boundaries

The primacy of the "animal" – the "desiring" – component in the human being, opens Hedonomat into the realm of what Freudianism terms "polymorphous perversity". Just as, in Freud's writing, the unformed child experiences bisexual desire, incestuous impulses and so forth, so the liberation of the essential (the pristinely animal) human being must give expression to the morphing across boundaries. Indeed the human is here accorded a freedom which the animal does not possess. Whilst generally the animal does not

---

13 *Isaiah* 55:8.

cross boundaries, human freedom, according to Hedonomat, is to be expressed in the social facilitation of "polymorphous perversity", the crossing of boundaries.

Two fundamental aspects of the untamed instinctual complex of the human being are sexuality and aggression. Civilization is supposed to sublimate and transform these instincts into constructive moral structures.

In the history of society, sexuality has been governed by the structure of marriage, and the system of permitted and forbidden sexual relationships. It is significant that under Hedonomat the boundaries of sexual morality have been broken primarily through the movement to vindicate homosexuality in society. No one will deny that homosexual impulses are part of the polymorphous perversity of the human being, and the impulse may be physically an extremely powerful one in certain individuals. But the boundaries established by morality, the concept of Divine purpose and function established by revealed morality, requires its containment and inhibition in actual practice.

Human aggression has been governed by civilization through concepts of justice and the use of force to back up legitimate authority and to punish breaches of justice. Without this discipline, power is a lust, like human sexuality. The raw concept of power is taken up in certain motivations of feminist demands, encouraged by Hedonomat, that equality requires that women find essential identity in taking up all the functions that men have traditionally fulfilled. There is nothing wrong (and everything right) with dignity and respect and fairness of treatment for women and the full deployment of talent wherever it is found. Financial autonomy and the ability to earn can protect women from dependency in abusive relationships. Nevertheless, features of this outlook have actually denatured the distinct and unique qualities of the female *vis-à-vis* the male where the driver is the *desire* for power and the status object is the essential *command* of resources and people. It has led to the devaluation of the

unique nurturing role of the woman in the family. It has denigrated
the function of the woman as a harmonizing force and moral
shaper of her family and children in favour of the notion of her as
a corporate power-wielder. Hedonomat thus through promotion of
homosexuality as co-normative produces the feminisation of the
male and through an unbalanced feminism the masculinization of
the female. It blends the boundaries between animal and human in
an environmentalism which relativises the value of human life and
negates the distinct role and purpose of the human within nature
(which does not entail the despoiling of nature or gratuitous cruelty
to animals).

The discussion of values

Restoring public discussion of ultimate values

The philosophy and practice of Hedonomat has been successful
in overriding the expression of the grass-roots religiosity of the
majority in the publics of western societies. Religion and the concrete
values which religion espouses have been driven into retreat. This
is evident not only in the area of sexual morality, in which biblically
and throughout the history of civilization fundamental prohibitions
on adultery, homosexuality, incest and bestiality prevailed. A concept
of marriage existed, which meant the permanent designation of
a spouse: this has been significantly eroded by a significantly less
committed *de facto* culture, which in England, for example, sees one
out of two children born out wedlock – producing a parentless
and family-less generation – with indescribable consequences for
youth violence, substance abuse and promiscuity. Hedonomat has
promoted much of this, with its primary emphasis upon personal
gratification, starting with parents who are not prepared to take upon
themselves the commitment and consequences of childrearing.

Hedonomat is big also on areas deemed by the religious tradition
to be killing. It favours abortion on demand (beyond justifiable

grounds such as danger to the mother's life), and it favours euthanasia because it does not know of the life of the soul, and the spiritual value of life. Hedonomat can also promote a culture of greed and theft, not only on account of its materialistic culture, but also for the simple reason that the child or adult can ride a train without paying because "no one" (not the conductor and not G-d, Hedonomat teaches) is watching. Hedonomat can corrupt justice with charters which free judges from tradition and policy based on deep social resonance to their own sense of justice. And needless to say in the realm of belief in, and respect for, G-d, it has mounted its greatest assault.

There can be a return to the true discussion of values, only when the elites which circumscribe the public discussion of values, are themselves forced into a social moral accountability. First of all, the staffing of all Government funded non-political entities of social influence must reflect a true plurality of standpoints, including religious ones. This includes bodies such as the Law Reform Commission of Victoria and the Australian Human Rights Commission. State owned media, such as the ABC, need to be scrutinized for political and ethical orientation. Secondly, the trend to establish charters of human rights must be minimized as they may encrypt ethical assumptions (very often those of Hedonmat) and then hand over their interpretation and application to individual judges, who with serious consequences, can change the course of publicly resolved social policy. The personnel of non-political policy elites, as well as this kind of conduct of judges, should be as open to public criticism as any politician.

There needs to be vigorous demythologisation of Hedonomat within the Universities. For academic staff themselves, this calls for an ethic of honesty and courage of personal conviction. No one should be afraid to criticize the values of a Professor, to whom respect can be due only on account of intelligence and work, not to any *a priori* claim, as "Professor", to moral rightness. The public must become that place where no one is afraid of, or ridiculed for, mentioning the name of G-d or values which traditional religion has associated with G-d. Above all what is needed is a demythologisation of "public reason", which excludes moral and other knowledge derived from the religious traditions. We must come back to a public, which is precisely that: a space, in which one is freely able to speak about the *first principles* of human conduct and knowledge.

Deprivatisation and demarginalisation of religious life

Hedonomat's version of the separation of religion and state has been, as noticed, to declare the public space, the space of public and state institutions, as one which precludes religious values, and to drive religion into a private space. Religion is acceptable so long as it has no impact upon policy and does not intrude into public institutions. Not only this, Hedonomat holds that religion may not be able to create its own moral environment within its *own* institutions. This is the import of a recent "Options paper" to revise the exceptions provided for in the Victorian Equal Opportunity Act for religious schools. The paper proposes to allow religious schools to select their Staff by their own criteria only in regard to the personnel *actually teaching a religious subject*. Other staff members in the school environment should not be subject to the criteria of the school. Accordingly, for example, an overtly practising homosexual maths teacher may have to be taken by the school, even though this conduct contradicts its ethic. In other words, the school may not model its own ethic through its staffing.

Thus an article published by the author of the Options Paper makes a spurious distinction between the private and the public life of religion (an assumption which runs through the Options paper). Religion can be tolerated in a private sphere of worship, but it must defend and justify itself when it assumes a public activity such as education. This is because in the view of Hedonomat, the public sphere cannot brook religious values. It has been staked out only for Hedonomat.

The attempts to force a retreat of religion into a private space where religion is no longer "lived" and practised as an integral lifestyle are fortunately challenged by section 19 (1) of the Victorian Charter of Rights and Responsibilities, which provides:

> All persons with a particular cultural, religious, racial or linguistic background must not be denied the right in community with other persons of that background to enjoy his or her culture, to declare and practice his or her religion and to use his or her language.

The same issue arises with regard to the entitlement of a religious community to live in an environment which resists forms of commercialisation such as nightclubs and sleazy culture or even overt offensive, suggestive advertising. The public square belongs as much to its religious constituents as to its non-religious constituents, and it has to be liveable for everyone. In other words, the "public" cannot be seized and regulated as a non- or anti-religious domain. The schools, the Parliament and the streets belong as much to, and must be as congenial to, religiously minded individuals as to those who are not. Government funding may not be withheld from religious schools with the argument that "the Public domain is not religious". To say this is to drive vast constituencies out of the public sphere.

Coercion against the expression of conscience

Hedonomat has succeeded in various domains in achieving coercion in an unexpected *qualitative* measure. One may argue that a group, which by claim of personally held values wants to practice harm to others, should not be allowed that expression of values. In such a case, one may force a group to *desist* from carrying out its values. However, in the form Hedonomat has taken in contemporary Victorian abortion legislation, it forces individuals *actively* to commit crimes against their consciences. Thus Abortion legislation enacted in Victoria in 2008 compels doctors either to perform an abortion or refer to another who will carry it out. This means that if the religious tradition of a doctor deems a particular abortion of a foetus as a case of prohibited killing, the doctor is compelled to one of two choices. One is to perform the abortion and directly transgress a severe moral prohibition. The other is to cause the death of the foetus by referring to another doctor who will perform the abortion. Both are transgressions against religious principle in an extremely serious matter. The doctor must act against conscience.

A second measure of Hedonomat is to foreclose discourse by linguistic (and possibly also legal means). There is a danger that speech will move from an etiquette of political correctness and silencing to political repression and punishment. The suffix "phobic" already demonises and pathologises attitudes not held to be politically correct. Criticism of the practice of homosexuality, and its institutionalisation as co-normative in society, becomes "homophobia" – censurable and potentially (under certain entertained legislation on hate crimes and hate speech) punishable.

Hatred based on racial prejudice is reprehensible, and society should do everything it can to educate against it. Nevertheless, it may be that legislation which makes "hatred" directed towards certain characteristics a crime or an aggravating factor can contribute worse dangers. The principal danger is that such legislation will become a new instrument of coercion and repression based on the ideology of Hedonomat. This will be particularly so if hate crime law is used by those who are ideologically opposed to the teachings of traditional religion to prohibit speech critical of sexual behaviour prohibited by religious tradition. The Canadian law C-250, passed in 2003, included sexual orientation as an area to be protected against speech construable as "hate propaganda". Even though an amendment was passed to the bill, which created "a defence from prosecution for opinions expressed 'in good faith' or based on a belief in a religious text" like the Bible, this has been reviewed by some critics as an irrational exception.

This exception had already been ironed out by a Swedish bill in 2002 (finally made law in 2003) which criminalized "hate speech" against protected groups including persons of varying sexual orientations, including homosexuals. A prosecution of a Christian minister resulted with a conviction which was subsequently overturned on appeal. What this shows is that even where criticism is levelled on biblical and religious grounds against the *practice* of homosexuality, it may be prosecuted on the grounds of "hatred" towards a "protected group".

There is a real danger that were this "hate crime" legislation (or its import in a particular bill of rights) to be introduced in Australia (with hate speech against racial groups very easily being extended to other groups such as those with different purported sexual orientations) it would not be with any of the tenuous "mercies" of the Canadian amendment or the Swedish court which overturned the conviction.

We live in a time of powerful contrast between two philosophies: one which believes in G-d and in a transcendent, an objective and an enduring morality; the other which does not believe (or suppresses its belief) in G-d, and allows the morphing of values and moral institutions in accordance with a purely materialistic calculus of pleasure and pain.

To resolve this conflict, we must come to a time when first principles are exposed and openly addressed. We need a public discussion in the most open and freest sense to check the true resonance of values. We need to remove all privilege from specific centres of influence – be these bureaucratic, academic or media – whether this privilege arises from their objective insulation from answerability to the public and political arena; or where the insulation has arisen from persons' own subjective deference to "political correctness". The building of understanding and the formation of a social consensus, to the extent that such is possible, can be done only where the "public" is the space where values are freely submitted to consideration; where individuals can openly live, teach and exemplify their values, where no coercion, policing of speech or action forces conscience against itself; where every piece of legislation, every proposal of "rights", is laid bare in its most pristine assumptions and values; and where the word "G-d" can be heard as openly, loudly and freely as the word "rights".

2
THE LEGISLATIVE STRUGGLE

The following critiques of legislative bills were sent to the Victorian Parliament in a deeply turbulent legislative period in 2008. In these bills, legislation was set forth to challenge (1) the concept of marriage, (2) the protection of nascent life, and to establish (3) new concepts of parenthood and childhood. All of these bills, at variance with traditional, universal Biblically based principles (the Noahide laws) were passed. A bill on voluntary euthanasia, presented also that year, was defeated.

The Relationships Bill 2008 and the Judicial Pensions Bill 2008: redefining marriage

Introduction

In his speech, upon the second reading of the Relationships Bill[14], the Victorian Attorney General (reported in Victorian *Hansard* 6 December 2007) indicates that the driving motive behind the Relationships Bill is the satisfaction of demands made by the homosexual lobby in Victoria. Even though the Information Paper

---

14 The *Relationships Bill* (2008) has the purpose (a) to establish a relationships register in Victoria for the registration of domestic relationships; (b) to provide for relationship agreements; (c) to provide for adjustment of property interests between domestic partners and the rights of domestic partners to maintenance; (d) to repeal Part IX of the Property Law Act 1958 and make consequential amendments to other Acts."

"A Relationships Register in Victoria", issued by the Victorian Department of Justice in May 2007, stated the Premier's intention as being to "establish a relationships register based on the Tasmanian model in Victoria", the Attorney General has limited its goal to a specific objective. The Tasmanian model includes *both* conjugal, sexually-based, relationships, and non-conjugal relationships, such as those of carers with those for whom they care. The Victorian Bill, however, deals exclusively with the former, fashioning it essentially as a vehicle for homosexual marriage in all but name, as will be explained. The name "marriage" is withheld since only the Commonwealth, under the Constitution, can make laws regarding marriage, which is defined in the Marriage Act as "the union of a man and a woman to the exclusion of all others, voluntarily entered into for life" (*Marriage Act 1961(Cth)*, s 46(1)).

The Intent and Structuring of the Bill

At present, the difference between marriage and de facto relationships in Victorian law is principally in two areas (1) property settlement upon break-up and (2) spousal maintenance upon break-up. Marriage partners upon break-up achieve a settlement based not only on a retrospective view of their contributions but also based on their prospective needs. De facto partners upon break-up can achieve a settlement based only upon their contributions in the past, not on their prospective needs. Marriage partners can apply for spousal maintenance. De facto partners cannot apply for spousal maintenance (other than birthing expenses and maintenance for some months prior to and after giving birth). The children of both marriages and de facto relationships, which have broken up, are entitled to maintenance.

The law establishing the distinct identity of de facto relationships in regard to property settlement upon break-up is contained in Part IX of the Victorian State Property Law Act of 1958. The laws providing for spousal maintenance for marriage partners after break-up are contained in the Commonwealth Family Law Act of 1975. The present Relationships Bill seeks to repeal Part IX of the Property Law Act, essentially making property settlement after break up identical for both married and de facto partners. It is intended to bring all (non-married) de facto partners, whether registered under the proposed Relationships Register or not, under the Relationships Bill, with its provisions as set out in part 3 of the Relationships Bill "Property and Maintenance".

This part of the bill provides for property settlement, which allows for adjustments in settlement, taking into account *future* needs, caused by the division of property (along marriage property settlement lines). Sections 51 and 52 of the bill also make provision for spousal maintenance upon the break-up of a de facto relationship modelled on the Commonwealth Family Act's provision for application for spousal maintenance upon the break up of marriage partners.

Thus the new bill changes the Victorian law of de facto relationships, modelling it substantially upon marriage. This is the only way a homosexual de facto couple could under State law achieve the practical status of marriage (without the name). A heterosexual de facto couple could achieve the practical status of marriage by simply getting married, something available under the Constitution and Commonwealth law only to a man and woman. All that would be needed now (under the present Bill) for a homosexual couple to achieve the practical status of marriage is to have their relationship registered. In the words of the "Relationships Tasmania" website[15], "registering a relationship in Tasmania creates a new legal relationship in exactly the same way as a civil union or a marriage". The same is envisaged for Victoria.

The Tasmanian website also notes that a homosexual couple may accompany their registration with their own vows, which could presumably also include a statement of commitment to one another for life, just like marriage. Essentially all that is absent is the word "marriage".

---

15 www.relationshipstasmania.org.au

Human rights and moral values

The Attorney General of Victoria in the Second Reading of the Bill states that this bill is based on human rights, as expressed in the Charter of Human Rights and Responsibilities. The question which is ignored here is whether a person has a right to do something which an objective universal ethics deems as immoral or departing from the moral norm. A society which deems the incestuous relationship of two siblings (or of a parent and child) as immoral withholds a "right" of the siblings to marry. There are no rights to transgress normative social morality. The ACT Civil Partnerships and the Tasmanian Relationships Act will not allow a brother and sister to register a relationship. The Victorian Relationships Bill makes no express limitation on relationships. It does not exclude incestuous relationships just as it does not exclude homosexual relationships on its Registry, with their legal status tantamount to marriage.

Even if this bill is to be read concurrently with the amended Crimes Act, section 44, which continues to criminalize even consenting to incest, and so would exclude incestuous couples from the proposed relationships register, still we have a question. The same Biblical tradition with which, according to the last Census, some 70 per cent of Australians are affiliated, states homosexuality and incest to be equally contrary to the moral, Divinely given norm. Why should we extend quasi-marital status and legal bolstering to a homosexual relationship any more than to an incestuous union, both prohibited from the same source?

This is also the systematic problem of the Human Rights and Equal Opportunity Commission's (HREOC) report "Same Sex: Same Entitlements". It starts with the *assumption* that there is a "right" of homosexuals to marry and acquire children by IVF or other means, and consequently produces a very large report with some "58 federal laws which discriminate against same-sex couples and their children". If it would similarly assume that there was a "right" of siblings, or of a parent and child, to marry, it would come up most likely with something like "58 federal laws which discriminate against incestuous couples and their children". The reasons are the same: the law embodies a moral principle that neither homosexuals nor siblings (or parents and children) are allowed to marry, and therefore in neither case legally recognizes such unions in respect of these laws.

This critique of the Relationships Bill does not imply a lack of compassion for people with homosexual practices. According to the religious view a human being has a soul, a mind and a body. Homosexual impulses, sometimes strong ones, can originate from the physical and mental makeup of a person. The essential identity of a human being however is the soul or spiritual identity (some call it "conscience"), and the soul is not homosexually inclined, since it resonates with the will of its Creator, Who, according to the traditions of the great historical religious faiths of humanity, has prohibited homosexual practice. Rather homosexual impulse, like any other contrary impulse emerging from body or mind, is something with which the essential person, the soul (which *has* a body and mind), must grapple and at least control, with the care, compassion and help of others.

If "homophobia" means fear or hatred of homosexuals, the religious view is certainly not homophobic. Rather, it wants to remove a social endorsement of homosexuality such as giving it the functional equivalence of marriage. Ultimately this removal of endorsement of homosexuality is for the benefit of homosexuals themselves. For if government and institutions teach that homosexuality is normative (as in this Bill), like heterosexuality, then it makes homosexuality a socially supported and sanctioned fate or destiny. There is no moral compass held up to help the homosexual, who desires to emerge from homosexuality. Beyond that, it teaches the young, who are sometimes uncertain of their sexuality, that homosexuality is as normal as heterosexuality (as we see already in some primary educational materials). It thereby cultivates and increases homosexuality in society. Government must be wary of uprooting authentic historical moral traditions, and relativising social institutions such as heterosexual marriage, to please activists of a group, whom such "reforms" paradoxically harm rather than help.

The Judicial Pensions Bill

The proposed Judicial Pensions Bill proposes to extend the pension, currently due to the spouse of a deceased Judge, to a homosexual partner. In so doing, it attempts once again to equate homosexual and heterosexual marital relationships, and should be judged in the same way as the Relationships Bill. To pass it, is simply to create precedents for the full scale equation of homosexual relationships and marriage in every remaining respect. When Justice Michael Kirby requested this bill at the Federal level for his own private purposes, the then Attorney General of Australia rightly responded on ABC radio, "I don't think it would be appropriate to deal just with high-profile High Court officers in isolation from the broader question [of law bearing on homosexuals]".

Responding to the genuine concerns of the Relationships Bill

In order to address the genuine concerns addressed by the Relationships Bill, it is important to recapitulate briefly the central objection to the Relationships Bill.

Marriage is the committed sexual union of a man and a woman, uniquely associated by the law with (amongst others) the obligation of the parties to provide for one another both during and *beyond* the marriage. This is reflected both in spousal maintenance and in the nature of the division of property upon the termination of the marriage, namely that it takes into account the *future* needs of the spouse.

Same-sex unions, within the category of de facto unions generally, are presently covered by the Property Act. In the Property Act, the sexual union *there* indicates an implicit *contractual* relationship between the parties in regard to their commonly acquired property and its division upon break-up. The uniquely marital commitment to provide for one another consistently during the relationship[16] and to provide for one another after the termination of the relationship, through a division geared also to *future* needs, are not expressed for de factos (including homosexual couples) in law.

The Relationships Bill takes provisions from the Property Act for de facto relationships, including same-sex relationships (which cannot be treated under the Commonwealth Family Law). It then joins these with key features of the Commonwealth Family Law Act – future-oriented property division and spousal maintenance – in a new Bill. This effectively makes the existence of a de facto heterosexual or homosexual relationship the *basis* of quasi marital obligations and entitlements.

This is to be opposed, since it invests a homosexual relationship with the significance of marriage. That the word "marriage" is not used in the new Bill, is of minor significance in view of the functional equivalence of marriage which it seeks to establish for homosexual couples. No marriage-style entitlements should be predicated on the existence of a homosexual relationship, since this mimics and so undermines the concept of marriage.

An element in the overall concept of the Relationships Bill, as was *originally* proposed by the Government in its Information Paper in May 2007, was the recognition of the neediness of people in a considerable variety of relationships, of which caring relationships are an example. People in such a relationship through the legal bolstering of this relationship, afforded by the Bill, could be justly served in various financial and work-related entitlements, access to the Medicare and PBS (Pharmaceutical Benefits Scheme), safety

---

16 Beyond the birthing expenses and a few months maintenance before and after birth, in which *de factos* are obligated, as noted above.

nets, tax concessions, access to superannuation accumulations and workers compensation death benefits, pension entitlements and access to aged care.

A solution to these genuine concerns originally intended by the Relationships Bill is to set up a register for relationships, which totally omits any criterion of sexual union for the establishment of the relationship. In the words of Professor Robert George (Princeton University), addressing the issue of relationships registers in the USA, this should have "nothing to do with whether the partners share a bed and what they do in it".[17] The relationship must be contracted on other grounds, all of which might be different aspects of "interdependence". This could be of a caring nature (such as an invalid with his or her carer), or of a financial or household nature (such as two brothers or sisters, or a parent and child). Even homosexuals who want to avail themselves of this, would have to establish their interdependence on grounds other than sexual union. Then, as a matter of registered and contracted interdependence, not on account of a sexual union, the parties could access special future-oriented provisions for property division and maintenance such as one finds in marriage. Similarly if the Government wants to allow a Judge's pension to pass after the death of the Judge to someone other than the Judge's spouse, that should be on grounds of interdependence between the Judge and that person. That interdependence is not to be established on the grounds of a sexual relationship, but rather in a caring, financial, household etc context, within parameters accepted by the Government for the transfer of the pension.

In summary, the Relationships Register should be a Register of acceptable "interdependencies", with all the benefits with which they can be justifiably endowed. The Property Act can be left intact and separate. It should make no reference to a sexual relationship as a foundation for the interdependency. This way many humanitarian

---

17 Robert P. George, "Law and Moral Purpose", *First Things*, January 2008.

needs would be satisfied. There is no need to undermine marriage by creating an equivalent of it, based on a same-sex sexual relationship.

Conclusion

(1) Marriage as a legal reality, and not simply a word, can morally only be established between a man and woman. It may not be enacted *or replicated* for same sex couples.

(2) Rights and claims of discrimination do not apply to the commission of acts which are deemed immoral or non-normative. Thus, there is no right of homosexuals to marriage, with all the attendant entitlements, any more than to incestuous marriage. Both are equally prohibited by the Biblical tradition.

(3) There are genuine grounds for contracting a supportive legal relationship between two interdependent people, but not upon the *basis* of a same-sex sexual relationship.

The Abortion Bill 2008: redefining the permission to take life

Law, values and social consequences

Within the framework of the Noahide laws – the biblical covenant enjoining all humanity, i.e. the descendants of Noah – endorsed by the American Congress in 1991 as "the bedrock of society since the dawn of civilization", is a prohibition on killing. Abortion can be a form of prohibited killing. Even though the foetus is not the same as a fully independent human being, and is dependent upon its mother, the Bible contains a verse, stating the wrongdoing of "Whoever sheds the blood of a person *within* a person"[18], which is traditionally interpreted to refer to abortion. The significance of

---

18 Genesis 9:6.

this injunction additional to murder is that *whether or not* the life of an unborn foetus is considered like that of an independently living human being, there is also a biblical stricture against feticide which is as stringent as killing an independent human being. There are, however, specific grounds upon which the life of a foetus can be taken, just as there are (exceptional) conditions under which other human life may be taken.

In the case of abortion, not only are parents and their agents – i.e. doctors – responsible for what they do, but also Governments. Law expresses values and establishes norms of social conduct. Legislators have to ponder those values. Legislators must also be mindful of the consequences of legislation for society. This study on abortion examines the moral, social and cultural implications of legislating abortion on differing grounds – including abortion requiring no grounds at all, namely abortion on demand.

Abortion on demand

The values implicit in legislation, which provides abortion on demand, are that the foetus is the property and part of the body of a woman *and* that she (or perhaps both biological parents) has (have) complete jurisdiction over it. Significantly it was the Soviet Union and Communist societies which extended abortion on demand as a basic principle. It is fundamentally consistent with a materialist philosophy, of which Communism exemplified one kind, and the hedonistic materialism found in currents of contemporary Western society is another.

This materialist philosophy, in its various strains, does not recognize the existence of a soul, which constitutes the innermost integral being of a person, whether dependant on another (like a foetus), sick, aged, disabled or healthy. The soul is entrusted by G-d, and together with the body and mind, which together form its vehicle, is no one's arbitrarily disposable property. The argument that the foetus is part of a woman's body, which she may *therefore* dispose of, like a benign (or not so benign) "tumour" contains a double mistake. Not only may she (or the parents) not dispose of this life, she (they) may not even dispose of her (their) own life (lives). We may not practise active euthanasia on any one. We may not commit suicide nor assist suicide.

Abortion on demand officially subscribes to the philosophy, which negates the soul, and enters into a purely material calculus of physical and intellectual goods. This philosophy has a close kinship with euthanasia. In its totalitarian variants it has been associated with genocide. Fully installed, secular materialism abrogates the "rights" of the soul, most notably in the right of a foetus to live.

Abortion to save the life of the mother

There are grounds for taking life, according to universal religious, or Noahide, law. These include self-defence against mortal danger or the defence from mortal danger to another. Abortion can be justified on these grounds, when it is necessary to save the life of the mother by taking the life of the foetus. The preciousness of life is demonstrated in that it may be taken for the sake of life, to preserve the life of the individual or of society.

Abortion on grounds of physical health

Based on the previous principle, Noahide law allows abortion on the grounds of a threat to health, only where that threat could widen to a danger to life. Gestation and childbirth are traditionally something difficult for womankind, but "being scared of childbirth", listed as a significant reason for abortions[19], does not warrant abortion. Even bad health, serious as it is, is not grounds to take foetal life.

To the extent that the law of a society formally disallows abortion

---

19 In Selena Ewing, *Women and Abortion*, Womens' Forum Australia, 2005

except primarily where there is a threat to life, it is consistent with traditional, universal morality as expressed in Noahide law. Even if the law has turned a "blind eye" to social practice, which has in fact breached this legal norm, and abortion is prevalent, there is no argument to "bring the law up to date" with social reality. For the law here expresses a moral ideal, to which society should be returned. The point is to *repair* the social institutions and conditions, which bring about situations where abortion is sought (on grounds other than the above), not to *institutionalise* abortion as a mechanism to service (and thereby validate) undesirable trends. Let us now consider two broad categories of – or reasons for – abortion, on (1) economic and (2) social grounds. What cultural trends and values are upheld, when abortion is legally sanctioned on these grounds?

Abortion on economic grounds

Perhaps the most common motivation for abortion is that the birth of a child is felt to limit the prospects of the mother in terms of work, study and career. The same may be felt by the parents of the child together. They cannot "afford" a child or that the child will place a strain on household finances. There may also be a circumstance of poverty. The law presently does not recognize economic grounds, though in reality great numbers of abortions are performed for these reasons. The moral presumption here is that the life of an unborn child can be terminated to improve the material wellbeing of the parent(s).

The moral objection to this argument from Noahide law and religious tradition is that a life cannot be taken to improve the material prospects of others. But apart from this, what are the cultural implications of an economic rationale for abortion, were the law officially to validate it? The impact is both upon the individual and the society. At the individual level the message is that additional material prosperity is of more importance than caring for, nurturing, and educating another human life. It intensifies a materialist and consumerist ethic relative to the qualitative interest in human relationships for their own sake. It makes inconvenience, personal effort and material sacrifice intolerable. It makes individuals unwilling to care, at many levels (whether through housing or visiting), for their own aging and invalid parents. It potentially furnishes impetus, beyond this for "voluntary euthanasia", whereby elderly and infirm parents or others are persuaded that they are a "burden" upon their children and society and should be removed. Ultimately, it could be argued, the materialistic ethic, with its narcissism and devaluation of other-regard, rebounds to harm the couple, who aborted to secure their own material future and comfort. If and when their relationship shows signs of not working, the pain of the effort required to restore the relationship is also unacceptable. Abortion on grounds of material considerations alters the personal calculus of care for life and human relationships. The material maximizing stance, which takes abortion as a "cost", is a further distancing from the erstwhile understanding of a religiously educated humanity: that the gift of a life is infinitely more valuable than greater economic ease.

If the resistance to abortion on economic grounds poses a strong challenge for the individual or couple faced by actual poverty, then it has to be remembered that society has an obligation to share their plight – to provide for the material wellbeing of its constituents. Society should alleviate the poverty which makes a woman or a couple think of abortion. The welfare provided by Government needs also to be supplemented by the charity of community and private individuals. Society must acknowledge the stresses on families and individuals and alleviate them to an acceptable standard. Fortunately, our society is both capable and willing to do this. But the state must be careful (even implicitly) not to factor in abortion as a mechanism of maintaining economic standards.

Abortion on social grounds

According to Noahide law, foetal life cannot be taken because of the social circumstances of the mother or parents. Similarly, the life cannot be taken away on an argument that the child will be "unloved" or "unwanted". A parent should make every effort to love and want her or his child, but the prospect or possibility of failure to do so, does not furnish a ground for taking the life. A significant number of abortions are undergone by single women and teenagers, by people who are "too young", who would face the unacceptable prospect of being a single mother, whose "partner could not cope", and who for such and other reasons are pressured by her parents or by parents of the father of the child, to abort.

Were the law officially to recognize these reasons for abortion, it would in fact be servicing, legitimating and bolstering the trends which produce these claims for abortion. Government must ask itself the questions: is early teenage sexuality and promiscuity a desirable thing? Is the increasing range of less committed de facto relationships a normative context for having children? Is society interested in educating towards responsibility in sexuality (not simply as "safe-sex") but towards sexuality as an expression of love and/or procreative purpose in a committed relationship which is essentially that of marriage, and not as part of a culture of self-gratification? It takes courage for Government to answer "no" to the first two questions and "yes" to the last. It may be even more difficult for Government to educate youth to sexual responsibility in a profound sense, to educate couples to commitment and spouses to improve their relationships, so that abortion does not become a social solution to difficulties in either of these areas. Perhaps much of the requisite education must come from the home, from the community school, from religious affiliation. But at least Government should not foster cultures of sexual social irresponsibility by officially servicing them with abortion.

Regulating abortion in order to remove unsafe abortion

The argument that the State must officially regulate abortion to remove the dangers of unsafe abortion is analogous to arguments for the legalization and regulation of prostitution, or drug use. The argument that it will happen and therefore we must make it safe is deeply problematic in that it sanitizes a moral wrong. Indeed it goes on to institutionalise it with a host of undesirable (and often unexpected) consequences. Rather, Government must ameliorate, and educate to remove, the conditions and attitudes, of which abortion is a consequence.

The mental health of the mother

"Mental health" was given as the reason for 97.5% of abortions in the South Australian survey in 2002. From the analysis of *Women and Abortion* published by Women's Forum Australia, it would appear that this category is largely associated not with dangerous psychological conditions, but with the worried response to a range of unwanted economic and social outcomes. It is not an issue of "mental health" *per se*, which could be considered to warrant the destruction of foetal life.[20] Indeed, it rather raises the question: what kind of disturbance of mental health itself could really warrant abortion, and under what circumstances?

Even in the case of a pregnant woman with a psychosis or severe mental illness, one must distinguish again, perhaps, as to whether this condition is caused by the circumstances of the pregnancy; or whether the pregnancy contributes stress to a pre-existing severe mental illness. In the latter case, it may be that other psychological interventions can help. Some research indicates that women with pre-existing mental illnesses are not necessarily worsened in their

---

20 Indeed, some writing indicates that abortion is a *source* of psychological malaise in a significant number of women. See for example, T. Burke with D. C. Reardon, *Forbidden Grief*, Springfield: Acorn Books, 2002, 2007.

mental health by having a baby.[21] Furthermore, abortion, with its sense of grievous loss can itself be a source of mental illness presenting as depression or in other forms.

The Menhennit ruling[22] (current Victorian law up to the present legislation) paired the terms "danger to her life or to her physical and mental health" as grounds for abortion. Clearly if danger to physical and mental health is sufficient cause for abortion, does danger to life need to be mentioned? To make sense the two would have to be linked. Not only does an immediate actual threat to life warrant abortion, even a threat to physical or mental health – not constituting an immediate threat to life – *but which could eventually threaten the life of the mother*, is also contemplated as grounds for abortion. It is interesting to note that the case which formed the basis of the Menhennit ruling was working within a framework of threat to life, *into which* it drew concepts of harm to mental and physical health, as we find in the following account:

> In his statement of law, Judge Menhennit drew on the 1939 English case of R *v Bourne*, which concerned the prosecution of a surgeon for performing an abortion on a young woman who had been the target of a ferocious rape. In that case, Justice Macnaghten had given what he considered a "reasonable" interpretation of the meaning of preserving the life of the mother in these terms: if "the probable consequence of the continuance of the pregnancy will be to make the woman a physical or mental wreck, the jury are quite entitled to take the view that the doctor who, under those circumstances and in that honest belief, operates, is operating for the purpose of preserving the life of the mother" (R *v Bourne* [1939] 1 KB 687, at 694).
>
> The phrase "preserving the life of the mother" has, on the basis of this precedent, been interpreted in a broad sense. For example, Justice Macnaghten noted that it was not always easy, or even necessary, to draw a line between health and

---

21 See *Women and Abortion* section 8.2, pp. 31-32
22 The ruling of Justice Clifford Inch Menhennit in R *v Davidson* [1969] VR 667.

life as being endangered, and he carefully noted that it was not necessary to wait until the woman's death was imminent before action became lawful on the stated criteria.[23]

In that, precedent case, a 14 year old girl had been gang-raped by a group of soldiers and the psycho-physical trauma of the resulting pregnancy could be said to be something which would, in the overall picture, hasten her death, (whether through the possibility of suicide or by some other means) and in the interim make her life a "living death". Thus the Menhennit ruling allows the reading that, to warrant abortion, a threat to physical or mental health (which is already present) had to pose a necessary and sufficient danger to the life of the mother, whether this impact will be delivered "imminently" or "eventually".[24]

The significant fact, however, according to the South Australian survey, is that *less than one percent of all abortions* are undertaken whether on account of threat to the life of the mother, or because of rape, incest or severe psychiatric disorders. This contrasts with the 97.5% of abortions, according to the same survey, which were attributed to "mental health", but in reality are due to economic and social reasons or general apprehensions, such as fear of childbirth. This broad interpretation of the words "mental health" can certainly not be used to justify the taking of foetal life.

Conclusion

(a) The terms of the Government brief of the Victorian Law Reform Commission, provide for two vastly different options: (i) for a decriminalisation of abortion, and (ii) for a legislative articulation of the Menhennit decision, namely a specification of the *conditions (only) under which* abortion may be performed. [In the event, the Parliament

---

23 Helen Pringle, 'Who's confused", www.Onlineopinion.com.au, 23 August 2007.
24 At all events there is a leniency in Noahide law with regard to abortion in the first 40 days from conception, which could be applied in cases such as rape and incest.

voted for the first option].

(b) Abortion is prohibited biblically (in Noahide law) as killing, even if the foetus is not fully identical to an independent human being

(c) The primary permission in Noahide law for killing a foetus (abortion) is in the circumstance where it endangers the life of its mother. (The trauma of rape or incest might also be grounds for abortion within the first 40 days from conception. Extreme malformation of the foetus, negating its ability to live, also warrants consideration).

(d) The Menhennit ruling can be given a limited reading consistent with the Biblical stance. Apart from its condition of danger to life, its condition of danger to physical and mental health, needs, however, also to relate to a danger to life, to warrant abortion.

(e) Government endorsed abortion on demand would carry the clear implication of non-recognition of the human soul as the innermost integral being of a person, with its claim to life. Such a secular materialism would overturn the faith traditions of 70% of Australians. It would have an essential kinship with voluntary euthanasia and assisted suicide teachings.

(f) Governmental authorisation of taking foetal life for economic or social reasons would not be merely morally and educationally wrong. It would also validate and foster the self-centred materialistic and consumerist culture, which puts personal gratification ahead of concern for others. It would also fortify a sexual culture of promiscuity, and an ethic of non-commitment to marry, both of which "require" abortion for their maintenance.

The Assisted Reproductive Treatment Bill 2008: redefining parenthood

The cultural impact of legislation

The Victorian Law Reform Commission, which has formulated proposals for legislation in assisted reproductive treatment, is a committee of private individuals. Their professional and expert qualifications do not *per se* endow them with moral authority, and for this reason they are required to engage in community consultations. Even after those consultations it may be found that for various reasons the opinions and the extent of the opinions of wide areas of Australian grass roots culture may not have been gauged in the actual recommendations and the legislation. Whether this was because of insufficient awareness or insufficient activism on behalf of bodies of opinion or for other reasons, we have a history of legislation (and proposed legislation), which could be said to have successively uprooted a series of long established values of Australian historical social culture and religious belief.

The law can (1) criminalize and prosecute a behaviour, (2) criminalize and not prosecute a behaviour and (3) decriminalize or legitimate a behaviour. If for various reasons, the law has chosen the second stage (to retain the criminalisation of certain behaviours but for practical reasons, or reasons of public interest, decided not to prosecute) this does not mean that it should proceed to stage (3) and legitimate it. This is because the legalization of the behaviour has vast cultural consequences. One example was the German institutionalisation of prostitution as a normal profession, with the consequence that a woman, who declined an employment offer as a prostitute was deprived of social security/unemployment benefits. This was a major social and moral reinforcement of prostitution. A second example, with the legislation of homosexual "marriage", where this has occurred, is the teaching in primary school curricula of the equal normativeness of homosexuality alongside heterosexuality. To legalize certain practices is to educate the society towards them as normative. In the words of Lord Devlin in the *Enforcement of Morals*, even if society does not prosecute immoral behaviour, *it may not condone it*. We would have to conclude from this that if it does condone it, the law is now teaching that this conduct *is* moral and normative.

In the following I wish to draw attention to the major problems associated with (implemented and proposed) IVF (In Vitro Fertilization) legislation, and the way they have conflicted with fundamental traditional moral principles of biblically based religion, with which, as the last census shows, the great majority of the Australian people are affiliated.

The 1984 legislation: obscuring the biological basis of parenthood

The Victorian IVF legislation of 1984 made possible the provision of IVF to couples in heterosexual marriage. Its novelty was to permit the use of donor sperm, i.e. sperm of a man other than the husband. This at once raised the issue of the identity of the father of the child. Biblical tradition speaks of a man and woman through marriage and procreation becoming "one flesh". *They* achieve their identity as one flesh through their child, and the child acquires *its* identity as the child of these parents. The spiritual and psycho-physical identity of parents and children are reciprocally defined through a *biological* relationship. Sensing the question of paternal identity which would arise, the 1984 legislation sought to deal with it by legislating away the parenthood of the biological father (the donor). This legislation permitted *bringing into being in the first instance* a child "without" a biological father to whom he or she could relate as such, something utterly different from the *after-the-event* situation of adoption, where a child was born with parents, but for whatever reason they could not keep their child. Subsequent developments have retreated from the attempt to "legislate away" the fatherhood of the sperm donor, by making this knowledge available to the child at a certain age; but the result is still a particularly fraught one.

The 1995 legislation: assisted procreation for unmarried parents

The 1995 legislation provided IVF as before, but now to couples in de facto relationships. The biblical concept of the union of man and woman (in which procreation takes place), assumes a fundamental mutual "designation" and commitment of the members of that union[25]. The de facto relationship does not correspond to the levels of commitment, as expressed in marriage, which society had taken upon itself until now to fortify the biblical norm of the union of man and woman (mutually committed, responsible and designated) in which procreation is to take place, and which affords fundamental contextual-familial security for children. This stage of the legislation educated towards de facto relationships as an acceptable norm and as an acceptable context for reproduction. Thereby it weakened the standard of the committed union of man and woman, which modern society had accomplished with the formal institution of marriage.

The proposed 2008 legislation: children without a mother and father

The proposed legislation wants to provide IVF for single women and lesbian couples and to provide adoption rights for homosexual

---

25 At the time this was written, the Relationships Bill had not yet been passed. The effect of the passing of the Relationships Bill (as described above) was to change the law of de facto relationships and to model the responsibilities and liabilities now associated with them, more closely on those of marriage. This does not mean, however, that couples living in a wide spectrum (in terms of degrees of commitment to one another) of de facto relationships will necessarily avail themselves of their entitlements and require each other to live up to their responsibilities under the new law, as they would during marriage or upon its dissolution.

couples. Through this it publicly validates sexual relations between people of the same sex, something forbidden by the Biblical norm, and establishes a same-sex relationship as the context for creating and raising a child. It also wants to employ surrogacy as a routine process, whereby parenthood will be further separated from its biological basis. Thus a "commissioning" couple (A and B) can take sperm from C and an egg from D and place the fertilized ovum in the womb of E. Once there was only a male donor and now there can also be a female donor. It is proposed, moreover, that both of them can be removed from actual parenthood of the offspring. The McBain decision (2000) determined, that IVF must be provided to single women and lesbian couples as a "right" to a service (which could not be withheld on account of marital status), contrary to existing legislation. The reasoning is identical to reports such as the HREOC (Human Rights and Equal Opportunity Commission) report "Same Sex: Same Entitlements", which *assumes* that a homosexual union is normative and that any law which does not facilitate it, as it would a heterosexual union, is discriminatory. But law does not have to extend "rights" to acts which it considers morally non-normative: it does not permit incest and does not regard any act which disadvantages an incestuous union in comparison to a permitted union, as discriminatory. The law, as it stood, permitting IVF for heterosexual couples only, was itself saying here that homosexual unions are non-normative and that they do not possess rights to IVF services just as they do not possess rights to adopt children. There is no need for Victorian statute to enshrine a judicial decision, which was based on a problematic extension of rights, at variance with the intention of the existing legislation itself.

Litigation and experience has forced IVF legislation around the world to face the fact that the bond of biological parenthood cannot be readily legislated away. The legislative response is to propose all kinds of "bandages", such as allowing children to know their biological parents and by permitting various composite listings of "parents" on a birth-certificate. The question remains: what right do adults have to "commission" the *production* of a child who will receive no nurture from its biological parents – to produce a child so radically emotionally, spiritually and humanly deprived? It is a good deed to adopt an orphan; it is not a good deed to create an orphan.

Summary

The Biblical ethic requires (1) that a child's identity is bound up, not only with its biological mother, but also with its biological father and that a child should be created in the first instance to be raised by its biological parents, (2) that children should be born to a mother and father who are committed to one another, up to the standards which civilization has generally accepted upon itself, namely marriage; and (3) that, apart from the moral non-normativeness of procreation by a single woman and of endorsement of a homosexual union, it is a deprivation of a child to create it without the prospect of being raised by a mother *and* father. The stages of past and proposed IVF legislation in Victoria have progressively encroached on each of these principles, the last of which (the current proposed legislation) is the most serious and the least defensible.

Submission to the Scrutiny of Acts and Regulations Committee (SARC) on the Assisted Reproductive Treatment (ART) Bill 2008

The provision of the charter

The *Victorian Charter of Human Rights and Responsibilities Act 2006* states in Part 2, section 17 ("Protection of families and children"):

(1) Families are the fundamental group unit of society and are entitled to be protected by society and the State.
(2) Every child has the right, without discrimination, to such protection as is in his or her *best interests* and is needed by him or her by reason of being a child.

Contravention of the child's best interests in the Assisted Reproduction Treatment Bill

IVF is a technology which can legitimately be used to help many people, particularly where it is used by mutually committed parents with their own gametes. But it is not a "service" which can "by right" be accessed by anyone, in any way, for any purpose. As an American Supreme Court Judge, Oliver Wendell Holmes Jr, said, "The right to swing my fist ends where the other man's nose begins". In this case the right of people to access ART stops at conditions which disadvantage a child born under these conditions. According to universal religious principles (Noahide law):

(1) An essential aspect of the identity of a person is the knowledge of who one's parents are.
(2) One's parents are one's biological parents.
(3) The biological parents are a man and a woman. Surrogacy creates ambiguities as to biological motherhood, namely as to whether the mother is the egg donor or the gestational mother. It is problematic, in terms of human identity, to create this ambiguity in the first place.
(4) A child's primary entitlement is to be raised by both his or her biological parents, mother and father.

Whilst IVF legislation already in 1984 allowed donor sperm (in IVF for married heterosexual couples) the latest Bill with its talk of "commissioning" a child (including the use of donor gametes and surrogacy) allows for the genetic concoction of a child to be taken home by people, to whom it bears no biological relationship whatsoever. The world has in it orphans, who lost their parents, or were given away by them. *After the event* that such a thing happens, it is a meritorious deed, where possible, to adopt such an orphan. It is a deep wrong, however, *in the first place to create* an orphan, as this Bill in fact seeks to facilitate (even with the fraught consolation that the child will be able to find out, through registries, who its biological parents are).

The disregard for the child's parental identity in this Bill is compounded by its ascribing of full normativeness to a homosexual setting as well as to conditions other than marriage or a legally reinforced de facto union for the raising of children (such as single mothers). Our common ethical tradition – through which the human soul has resonated with its Creator for thousands of years – regards these conditions, in the norm, as deprivation. Any purported "right" to the use of a service which results in the creation of a thereby disadvantaged child is no right at all.

Negation of the argument that no claim can be made because the embryo is not a person ("child") in the sense of the charter: the concept of "wrongful life".

The secular law recognizes concepts of "wrongful birth" (where typically damages are sought by parents on account of the birth, such as where a doctor mistakenly assessed the dangers of a pregnancy or performed a faulty vasectomy) and "wrongful life", where the child is a claimant. In other words, there is a concept in law that even at the point of conception, a misdeed can be said to have been committed which harms a living person of the future, i.e. to have brought harm upon, and infringed the rights of what will be a person or child, in the sense of the Victorian Charter. Such was the American case of *Zepeda v. Zepeda*[26], where the (adult) child appealed against his father who had conceived him in an adulterous relationship, granting him the status of illegitimacy. The court ruled that a *wrong*[27] had been perpetrated against the plaintiff, even though the court would not grant damages (for practical reasons, namely that the court would be flooded with such cases)[28]. That is to say, even where damages cannot be collected for wrongful life, a wrong may nevertheless be deemed to have been perpetrated at the point of conception or initial "production" (through IVF)

---

26 See http://www.law.duke.edu/shell/cite.pl?52+Duke+L.+J.+807#F33
27 *Ibid.*, footnote 33.
28 See the Australian law: http://www.austlii.edu.au/au/cases/cth/HCA/2006/15.html

against a "full" person, when this production was carried out to place the person who would result from this production in an ultimately disadvantageous situation (here, the placing a child in a circumstance without proper parenthood and identity). This finds resonance with the Biblical ethic, (subject to the highly restricted permission for abortion) with its recognition of conception as the potentiality of life.

Conclusion

(1) Parenthood, and conversely childhood, are biologically established.
(2) It is normative that children be born to parents in a committed relationship.
(3) It is an injustice to create a child without both a mother and a father.
(4) Legislation should recognize the harm done to a future person during its conception or in gestation in the legal concept of "wrongful life" (a *wronged* life established with IVF by "commissioning" individuals other than its biological parents).

Postscript

The SARC (Scrutiny of Acts and Regulations Committee[29]) Report No. 14 of 2008, p.3, with regard to section 17(2) (dealing with protection of the child) of the "Victorian Charter of Human Rights and Responsibilities", addressed and responded to some of the points made above in the following terms:

> The Charter also doesn't follow the *United Nations Convention on the Rights of the Child* in requiring that all decisions be made in the child's best interests. Rather,

---

[29] A Parliamentary committee established to examine consistency of legislation in the Victorian Parliament with the "Victorian Charter of Human Rights and Responsibilities" enacted on 25 July 2006.

it provides only a narrower right for children to such protection as is in their best interests <u>and</u> is needed by them 'by reason of being a child'.

No explanation was made of how the Victorian Charter in section 17(2) differs from the requirement of the United Nations Convention on the Rights of the Child, that "all decisions be made in the child's best interests" in concept and application of the principle of the "child's best interests". Without an explanation, it is not evident how SARC had considered several of the submissions, including that of the Institute for Judaism and Civilization. The expression of the committee – "Rather, it provides only a narrower right for children to such protection as is in their best interests <u>and</u> is needed by them 'by reason of being a child'" – remains quite unclear.

PART 2:
QUESTIONS FOR A UNIVERSAL
ETHICS

3
"RIGHT" AND "LEFT"
IN UNIVERSAL ETHICS

There is a natural diversity of human, and therefore also of political, "temperament". Terms such as "right" and "left" evoke such differences. Can a "natural" political diversity be accommodated within universal ethics? To answer this question we look first at a classic portrait of irreconcilable conflict in political thought between "individualist" thought, stressing the role of the individual, and "collectivist" thought emphasizing the role of the state. Some instances of this conflict are represented as an opposition of "right" and "left". From there we go to the actual tradition of universal ethics from Sinai to see how similarly distinct perspectives can *cohere* within a tradition of shared basic values. After that, we return to clarify the concepts of "right" and "left" which can coexist *within* the perimeter of universal ethics, taking that tradition into general political society.

Individualism and collectivism

Conflict in the secular tradition

In approaching the question of whether universal ethics can contain within itself a "natural" spectrum of "right-" to "left"-wing political temperaments, we turn to the history of political thought. Here we find an important divide between schools of individualism, on the one hand, and collectivism, on the other. In heightened form, the philosopher Karl Popper sought to explore this distinction in the difference between what he called open, democratic societies and their opposite, totalitarian societies, whether of the communist or fascist variety. In formulating such a polarity in political thought, he glosses over a spectrum which joins these two poles. Many forms of socialism, and particularly a democratic socialism, are not as extreme, closed and monolithic as the communist or fascist collectivist states. They are, however, believers in the primacy of the state as the agent of social justice and dispenser of the public good. Only the state, in this view, can effect social fairness and a proper distribution of wealth. The same moderate collectivist doctrines might also profess certain individual liberties, freedom of expression and conscience, but it is weighted towards the collective. Similarly, on the other side, stand a spectrum of social doctrines, which assert the primacy of the individual over the state, in graduated degrees, and seek to reduce (if not in the anarchist extreme, to eliminate) the role of the state.

In drawing this contrast between collectivist and individualist political philosophies, Popper was himself clearly and passionately on the individualist side of the divide. But it is useful to pursue Popper's analysis of the difference between the two paradigms, so that we might eventually in this chapter come to a neutral understanding of a basic spectral diversity in human political sentiment, consistent with universal ethics.

Grouping several philosophers of the collectivist camp (Plato, Hegel and Marx), Popper in his work, the *Open Society and its Enemies*[30], began to elaborate a paradigm of "holist" thought, with a variety of characteristics. He submitted this paradigm to intense criticism, from the vantage point of the second paradigm, an individualistic

---

30 London: Routledge and Kegan Paul, (1945) 1966, 2 Volumes.

"empiricism".[31]

Popper's contrast of these two paradigms can be philosophically reconstructed in three dimensions. The first – *metaphysical* – dimension relates to the issue of understanding objects in the natural, objective world. This has to do with the relationship of the empirical phenomena of the world before our eyes and their "objective" meaning and significance. This brings us to the philosophical distinction between "particulars" (individual phenomena) and "universals" (their general concepts or forms). Popper suggests that the adherence to a notion of universals, i.e. of forms representing an abstract idea, which subsume individual exemplars, is typical of holistic thought. Such was the view of Plato, who held that the world of empirical reality, for example, of particular chairs, trees and patches of colour is constantly changing. As such it has no ultimate "truth". Enduring and therefore also ultimately real and true are the "forms" of things, the concept of a chair, of a tree or of a particular colour, in short a realm of knowledge of "forms" or "universals" beyond physical reality. Aristotle, we could say[32], on the other hand, accorded value and meaning to the specific and individual objects of changing empirical phenomena. Plato, the holist (collectivist), relates and subordinates the individual phenomenon to its abstract idea or form. Aristotle, the empiricist (individualist), focuses upon the individual phenomenon as it is in the here and now.

The second dimension of comparison of holist and individualist-empiricist thought is *epistemological*, i.e. having to do with the nature of knowledge and explanation in the sciences. Here, Popper focuses on the realm of human or social sciences, which German thought designated as *Geisteswissenschaften*, the sciences of the human culture and society. They are distinguished from sciences approaching the natural world *(Naturwissenschaften)* which look at physical nature,

---

31 See pre-eminently chapter 5 of *The Logic of Scientific Discovery*, London: Hutchinson, 1959.
32 Though Popper does not characterize or contrast Aristotle's thought to Plato in this way. I am indebted to Professor I. Bloch, Professor emeritus of philosophy at the University of Western Ontario, London, Canada, for discussion of this point.

including the physical nature of human beings in the sciences of medicine and human biology. The human and social sciences study realms of action of the human being, where the power of choice, and the human ascription of meaning and value is important. Popper focuses the conflict of holism and empiricism in their treatment of the human sciences. Here Popper again chose to characterize and attack holism by finding in it "an approach to the social sciences which assumes that *historical prediction* is their principal aim, and which assumes that this aim is attainable by discovering the 'rhythms' or the 'patterns', the 'laws' or the 'trends' that underlie the evolution of history"[33]. Here he had in mind particularly the "historicist" outlook of doctrines such as Marxism, which sees overpowering trends in history, presenting the inevitability of revolution. Popper opposes to this, his own empirical-individualist view that in the human, historical sphere, there is a dynamic multiplicity of interactions, which no overall law can express: "The real outcome will always be… the resultant of the momentary constellation of contesting forces… [and] the balance of forces is bound to change."[34] In summary the difference between the two paradigms in the dimension of change is that the holist-collectivist view contemplates and embraces radical social transformation; the individualist view of history recognizes and accepts piecemeal change.

Popper's characterization of the empiricist-holist or individualist-collectivist divide is expressed thirdly, in the *ethical* dimension, where conceptions of the *good* are set forth. In the *Open Society and its Enemies*, Popper seeks to connect a doctrine of moral uniformity with the holistic theories of Plato, Hegel and Marx. With their common focus on the state, the root of morality becomes the welfare of the state. In connection with Plato he writes that "'just' is used by Plato as a synonym for 'that which is in the best interest of the best state'. In short, "Plato considers justice not as a relationship between individuals, but as a property of the *whole state*, based upon

---

33 *The Poverty of Historicism*, London: Routledge and Kegan Paul 2nd ed'n, 1960, p. 3.
34 *Ibid.*, p. 47.

a relationship between its classes. The state is just if it is healthy, strong, united and stable."[35] Popper finds this position even more extremely stated by Hegel in relation to the Prussian state. He speaks of Hegel's "Platonism and his insistence upon the absolute moral authority of the state, which overrules all personal morality, all conscience".[36] So too, he rejects the legacy of Marx, whose followers disparaged "mere formal freedom" in their construction of a communist state[37]. In the holist or collectivist camp, the good of the individual yields to and merges with duty towards the state.

In reconstructing the individualist-empiricist position in ethics, Popper finds Aristotle exemplary. Aristotle's individualist concept of justice

> is not, as Plato would have it, the health and harmony of the state, but rather a certain way of treating individuals, …[as] emphasized by Aristotle…when he says 'justice is something that pertains to persons'[38]

In summary, holism-collectivism understands the political good as a good order of society as a whole; empiricism-individualism grasps the good as a good for individuals.

A neutral concept of the collectivist-individualist divide

Popper's contrast of collectivist and individualist thought served a clear, personal purpose: to identify and reject forms of collectivism, especially the communist and fascist regimes he witnessed in his own life. His methodological distinction between collectivism and individualism is valuable, but its use is blocked by the specific values or doctrines he associated with it. According to his examples of collectivism, it is an irredeemable doctrine. To see, however, whether individualist and collectivist philosophies other than the

---

35 *Ibid.* p. 90.
36 *Ibid.*, Vol 2. p. 31.
37 *Ibid.*, Vol. 2, p. 127.
38 *Ibid.*, Vol. 1, pp. 101-102

ones he represented can be upheld and moreover cohere within the framework of universal ethics, we need to understand the divide more neutrally and dispassionately. Their difference can be reformulated as follows.

In general, in political terms, the difference between collectivist or holist thought and individualist-empirical thought has to do with the relationship of "whole" and "part". The collectivist standpoint says that the individual gets his or her essential definition in terms of the systematic relationships or structuring of the whole. That is, the ordering of the whole essentially defines the individual as a part of *its* order. The individualist outlook on the other hand, sees the whole as *arising out of* the constitutive activities of individuals. For the collectivist, the whole is constitutive of the individual; for the individualist, individuals are constitutive of the whole. One writer has summarized it thus:

> Is the whole a collection of entities, details found together, a structuring arising out of their being together, so that even within the generality, the detail does not lose its distinctness? Or, are the details engendered from the differentiation of the whole, so that the whole is a constitutive relationship, and within the whole the detail is not an independent entity?[39]

In its application to politics, this formulation needs modification. Most views would sit somewhere along the spectrum between the two poles. Many collectivists will give *some* autonomy to the individual; and many individualists will acknowledge the reality of the state, to some degree, as a reality "of its own" beyond moment-to-moment remaking by its constituent individuals. Nevertheless, with this difference of emphasis between the individual and the whole, one can frame the three dimensions of comparison between individualist and collectivist philosophies more neutrally; without the animus of

---

39 Rabbi Moshe Grossberg, *Zephunot HaRogatchovi*, Jerusalem 5718, p. 9. Present author's translation.

Popper's writing against specific collectivist philosophies.

In political terms, the "metaphysical" question becomes: what is the greater reality, that of the individual or society? Is our primary focus on the individual human actor as the one who together with others is actually constitutive of society; or is it upon the organization of the state or society which *gives* the individual his or her significance *within* that order?

In the realm of epistemology, or specifically social explanation, do we understand historical movement as a dynamic of the whole, with overall trends; or is historical and societal change essentially "piecemeal" and full of contingencies? The former view could entertain revolutions, transformations and overall processes as the dynamic of social change. The second view, however, sees social change as the work in progress of individuals and smaller constellations of events.

Finally, in the realm of ethics, the collectivist view will measure individual circumstances against more abstract ideals which exist in tension with the individual's circumstances. The collectivist is more ready to posit an order of relationships representing social good and to impose upon the individual a concept of duty towards that order of relationships. The individualist view, on the other hand, does not see the individual so much beholden to duties which would limit his or her own "freedom", except not to harm others or infringe basic obligations. The individualist position is that benevolence to others cannot be purchased through (excessive) obligation to a higher social authority, and loss of personal freedom.

Set out as fundamentally opposed perspectives, but in a neutral sense, we can find many more exemplars of collectivist and individualist thought represented by Popper. We can proceed to view them as "natural" mindsets or temperaments, which feature also in contemporary western democracies, with a basic polarity between a major individualist-liberal party and a major social-collectivist labour party. The question now becomes whether these basically different political mindsets presenting a "natural" human political diversity can also find expression within the framework of *shared* universal ethics? To answer this question, we turn to the religious tradition of universal ethics from Sinai, in which the same issue arises and is resolved.

Unity and diversity in the tradition of universal ethics

Tradition and temperament

The tradition, which comes down from Mount Sinai at which the Ten Commandments were given, sets out two bodies of significantly overlapping moral precepts or laws. One is a body of 613 precepts binding the Jewish people. The other is a body of seven broad, universal precepts with many details, called the Noahide laws, after the survivor of the biblical Flood and father of general humanity, Noah. Everything in which a Gentile (a "Noahide" or descendant of Noah) is morally bound by this tradition, also binds a Jew.

As Divine revelation, these laws are eternal and immutable. At the same time we find a variety of positions on interpretation and application of these laws within the tradition, to the extent that one could even speak of "parties" or contesting approaches to the law. How is this multiplicity consistent with the notion of a unitary tradition of eternal laws? We can explore the answer to this question with regard to diversity of approach within the Jewish aspect of the tradition. Later we shall look at a comparable diversity within the tradition of interpretation of the Noahide laws.

When Divine Revelation – the revelation at Sinai, the law and the commentary on that law given at Sinai – "comes down" into the world (i.e. is received by human beings) it experiences a differentiated reception. This Law, which is G-d's "own" norm for the creation, is *one*. When, however, it comes into the different temperaments of individual teachers and scholars of the tradition, it is refracted into a multiplicity of perspectives within that tradition. This does not mean that *any* reception or interpretation of the Divinely given Text is acceptable. Only the interpretations by those persons, who have been trained by teachers in the tradition and possess a profound receptivity to, and alignment with, the tradition, can reveal facets of it which are authentic facets of the Divine Law. Their differences and disputes are "for the sake of Heaven" and for that reason their differing views are facets *of the Divine Law*. These differing authorities do not dispute the *substance* of the Divine precepts. Rather, the differing spiritual personalities of Torah sages refract the light of the *one* Divine Law into different hues or nuances.

The fundamental concept of the human being as made in the image of G-d, helps to explain the concept of *spiritual* temperament or personality in recipients and interpreters of the tradition. In the mystical literature of the tradition, it is explained that the attributes of the human soul parallel the Divine attributes.[40] Just as there is a Divine attribute of "kindness" so there is an attribute of "kindness" in the human soul. The same applies to the attribute of "rigour" or "discipline". Whilst the Divine attributes are employed by G-d in a modulated harmony, it is characteristic of the human recipients of the tradition, that certain attributes should predominate in some individuals (or schools of thought) more than in others.

This is the explanation of the classic difference between two schools – the "House of Shammai" and the "House of Hillel" in relation to interpretation of the precepts of the tradition specifically binding Jews. As explained in mystical writings[41], the predominance in the spiritual personality of the House of Hillel of the Divine attribute of kindness *(chesed)* inclined them towards a more lenient interpretation of the Divine Law and to more lenient Rabbinic legislation which applies and installs it in the world. The Divine attribute of rigour or discipline *(g'vura)* predominating in the spiritual

---

40 As explained elsewhere, the Divine attributes do not inhere in G-d but are created and utilized by Him in His conduct of the creation.
41 In the "Compiler's Introduction" to the *Tanya* of Rabbi Schneur Zalman of Liadi.

personality of the House of Shammai, on the other hand, inclined
them to a more stringent interpretation of the Divine Law, and a
more stringent view of the Rabbinic legislation required to buttress
it. Whilst the tradition contains the truths of both the Houses
of Shammai and Hillel, Rabbinic adjudication determines their
introduction into the world at different times, or in simple terms
when the law will be in accordance with the House of Shammai or
with the House of Hillel.

The difference between the House of Hillel and the House of
Shammai has been explained as a difference of emphasis upon
"actuality" and "potentiality".[42] This can be elucidated in a general
sense with reference to a dispute between the two Schools over a
more mystical and symbolic question. The question, was what in the
process of creation, was created first, Heaven or Earth. The House
of Shammai maintained that Heaven was created first and the House
of Hillel, maintained that it was the earth. The significance of this
particular dispute has been understood to relate to the issue of which
shall be in the service of which. In other words, is it the purpose
of the spiritual realm ("Heaven") to be *drawn down* into the physical
creation ("Earth") – or is it the purpose of the physical creation
(Earth) to be *elevated* and attain to its spiritual source (Heaven)?[43]

We can translate this distinction into the philosophical dimensions
of the divide between individualism and collectivism. The House
of Shammai sees in the empirical, practical creation primarily its
deficiency in relation to the spiritual norm. The norm is beyond, and
the empirical world must set its sights on, and be elevated to model,
that norm. Consequently, it imposes a higher duty upon humanity to
transcend humanity's present limitations. With this it aims to close
the gap between actuality and potentiality, the concrete and the ideal
of perfection. The legislation of the House of Shammai accordingly
legislates a more rigorous regimen of conduct of the same set of

42 See Rabbi M.M. Schneersohn, *"Hadran al shisha sidrei mishnah"* in *Sefer HaSichot 5748*,
N.Y.: Kehot, section 26 *et passim*.
43 *Hadran, op. cit.* pp. 657-659.

precepts of the tradition, recognizing the fact of perverse human will, which needs extra controls.

For the House of Hillel, on the other hand, a different attitude operates. The good of the spiritual realm exists for the sake of the human being's worldly conduct, and this potential ideal has to be accomplished practicably in the actual. Accordingly, it is more lenient in its legislation of precautionary measures and additional requirements in fulfilment of the precepts of the tradition. Focussing on the *installation* of the Divine ideal into the concrete world of human particularity, the House of Hillel finds it must be more lenient in view of the limitations and space of the individual. The ideal is to be accommodated in practical reality, and that accommodation means "letting up" on a transcending intensity, for a less rigorous standard in the application of the ideal.

Another way of expressing this difference is that the House of Hillel is concerned with the way a Divine ideal is settled – "brought down" into this world, and the way each individual accommodates the ideal in his or her own concrete personality. The concrete and the individual is primary. For the House of Shammai it is the Divine ideal which is primary, to the expression of which this world must seek to ascend. The Divine ideal is of course emphasised in the concept of the oneness of G-dliness, and the society which seeks to express this must to some extent submerge the distinct and concrete individuality of its members, to achieve this harmony amongst themselves, as an expression of the Divine oneness.[44]

In truth, the tradition from Sinai requires that everyone must incorporate within one's own ethical life and service of G-d, *both* the transcending aspiration, characteristic of the House of Shammai *and* the practical this-worldly focus of the House of Hillel. The Divine will, after all, is that we should "ascend" to fetch the Divine ideal and then "descend" to bring it into this world. One without the other is a deficient service. While both the transcending ideal

---

44 See sichas parshas Vayakel in *Toras Menachem 5752* NY: Kehos.

and its installation into practical reality pertain to everyone (to both Shammai and Hillel), nevertheless the spiritual-temperamental difference between Shammai and Hillel is their respective *emphases* on different sides of the process.[45]

The same idea can be expressed in the language of "individualism" and "collectivism". A *purely* collectivist outlook with all its idealism can end up treating individuals, with their practical differences, brutally. A *mere* individualism, without any ideal of the public good (i.e. without collective and mutual regard) can end up as free-wheeling selfishness. A moral society necessarily seeks both the public good and is sensitive to the individual. The moral citizen is thus both collectivist and individualist, but the political difference between moral citizens rests within the balance of collectivity and individual, whether they are focussed *more* upon the one or the other.

The tradition and the coherence of perspectives

Why is it that between the individualist secular doctrine of a Popper and the collectivist secular doctrine of a Marx, there is irreconcilable conflict, whilst the individualism of the School of Hillel and the collectivism of the School of Shammai recognized one another (and were recognized by the subsequent history) as belonging to the one tradition? The answer to this is that both Hillel and Shammai are oriented to a common source: the same G-d and the same Divinely revealed teaching. Within that Divine teaching, all the facets of the *same* law, the individual and the collectivist, the "kinder" and the more "rigorous" versions, cohere and coexist. Significantly, both Hillel and Shammai "received" the tradition from the same teacher (one generation closer to the source than they). In their teacher's mind both their subsequent, differing perspectives were modulated and harmonized. When the particular "vessel" of Shammai's spiritually

---

45 Indeed, the ultimate objective, to be realized in the Redemption, is that Divine transcendence be "housed" (manifested) immanently within the finite creation, uniting the standpoints of both the Houses of Hillel and Shammai.

informed intellect refracted a particular aspect of the Divine law, in accordance with the attribute dominant within Shammai, it could ultimately coexist, with the dominant attribute in the perspective on the law refracted by the "vessel" of Hillel's spiritually informed intellect. Objectively, they were "sides" of the one moral tradition and teaching received from their teacher. Even though *one* of these perspectives would prevail at a given historical time, the other could recognize and acknowledge it. Since in their spiritual source they were one, the specific aspects which they drew forth from the same source could also be united "down below"[46].

In the secular tradition, by contrast, where a Plato, a Popper and a Marx are not oriented *beyond themselves* towards the same source, but are guided by their own *selves*, i.e. their own predispositions and personal worldviews, values and interests, they come into inevitable conflict. When the "autonomous" secular self – acknowledging no shared transcendent source – comes to the fore, potentially *all* the parties come into conflict. *Different sources,* as first principles drawn from private dispositions and worldviews, feed into individualist and a collectivist temperaments. Then one party's "disposition" writ large into a holist teaching collides with the other's party's "disposition" similarly writ large into an individualist teaching.

When on the other hand, both temperaments receive from the same tradition – the same G-d and the same revelation – they become exponents of distinct facets or emphases of the one substantive law. Individualism and collectivism, take their admissible content from the Divine law, and accordingly become differing perspectives on the same law. As such they can then also cohere with one another and constitute a legitimate diversity within the Divine law. Judicious human guidance and choice will determine which perspective or emphasis on the same laws and values will prevail in the historical moment. This is the concept of a natural human political diversity *within* a harmonious and unitary tradition.[47]

---

46 See Rabbi M. M Schneerson, Maamorim of the year 5715, *Mattos.*
47 See *Tanya (Likkutei Amarim)*, ch. 8. On the foregoing see at length Rabbi Sholom DovBer Schneersohn, *"Vayigdalu hana'arim", Sefer HaMa'amarim 5665*, N.Y: Kehot, pp. 104-09.

"Right" and "Left" within universal ethics

"Right" and "left" in politics

Perhaps the most common terms, in ordinary language, for comparing political parties and their doctrines are "right" and "left". As simple and inadequate as these may seem they nevertheless contain a very important value and classificatory importance. This needs to be explored, with definitional adjustments and clarification, before proceeding to understand how a shared belief in universal ethics could at the same time incorporate a political diversity of "right" and "left".

We began by looking at a divide in the history of thought, by reference to a schema set out by Karl Popper, between individualist thought and collectivist thought. The exemplars of those two paradigms were presented, within the secular tradition, as being in fundamental conflict. From there we went to the tradition from Sinai, which is a unitary tradition, continuously subscribing to the same universal, objective values, but which also contains "parties" or differing schools of interpretation. These parties exhibited distinct "soul" emphases in the Divine attributes of "kindness" and "discipline". That is to say they represent essentially different *temperaments*, associated with those soul attributes, which present as slightly differently cast versions of the same precepts of the tradition.

Interestingly, these different temperaments or attributes within the tradition themselves relate to the terms "right" and "left". In the mystical *(s'firotic)* schema of the Divine attributes, the attribute of kindness is placed on the "right", whilst the attribute of discipline is placed on the "left". This would appear to conflict with the secular connotations of the terms "right" and "left". In the secular tradition, the parties of the left, typically parties of social change, would appear to be "kind" in their drive towards a radical social justice, whilst those of the right would seem to be "disciplined" in their greater concern for protection of the space in the *status quo* forged by individuals in the exercise of their own freedom.

In fact, it is the other way around in terms of the mystical aspect (and dimension of explanation) of the tradition from Sinai. This is explained in terms of the relationship between the spiritual ideal "above", and the human reality "below". "Kindness" (in the classic model of giver and receiver) bestows from above *to* the needy below. So too, Divine Kindness (as embodied in the legislative "angle" of the School of Hillel), makes allowance for the actual and practical limitations of human beings. It works with what humans "down below" can and do achieve and therefore seeks a more lenient ("kindly") accommodation of the Divine ideal with respect to the actual abilities of the individual. Divine discipline or rigour (seen in the legislative angle of the School of Shammai) on the other hand, requires of the person to "shape up" and ascend to conform with a more rigorous standard of duties to the Divine ideal, "above".

In social and political terms, the Divine attribute of discipline or rigour thus presses additional stringencies upon the human subject to raise his or her actual conduct towards the ideal of a perfected coexistence of individuals in an order of Divine truth. Divine kindness would seek to accommodate the ideal down below in the realm of individual human limitation, practical accomplishment and freedom. In this scheme, individualism is on the "right", just as Divine kindness is placed mystically on the right; collectivism is on the "left" just as Divine discipline and rigour[48] is placed on the left.

To the extent that they correspond to attributes of G-d and the human soul, and with different emphases, implement the same substantive values of the tradition from Sinai, there could be nothing pejorative in either of the terms, "individualism" and "collectivism". So too, in the world of general society and politics, both parties of the "right" and the "left" could form an acceptable diversity and coherence *within* a shared commitment to universal ethics. Before taking over concepts of "right" and "left" for universal ethics, let us first further clarify the schema of "right" and "left".

48 See *Likkutei Sichos*, Vol. 25, pp. 246-47 and Vol. 6, p. 78.

Objections to the "right"-"left" classification

The most common example of the right-left distinction in secular political parlance, is the capitalist-socialist distinction. Capitalism, on the "right", stresses the primacy and freedom of the individual to build one's own particular world and future. Socialism, on the "left", anticipates a perfected world, in which all individuals have been harmonized into a cooperative order. Its method of achieving this is, practically, through state direction. The same polarity exists in more moderate forms. In most democratic societies today "capitalist" parties no longer advocate undiluted *laissez faire* capitalism, but accept and even affirm a degree of state regulation and welfare. Similarly, today "socialist" groups have often become "social-democratic" parties, which, alongside state administration and oversight of welfare, acknowledge a basic scope of individual freedom both in terms of personal expression and the individual's permission to create a personal "estate". The difference is in the degree of "size" and regulatory role they would accord to Government. The magnitude of taxation is of direct relevance here.

Putting *all* political thought, however, into one of the categories of individualist or collectivist thought, and calling these respectively right and left, seems patently to overlook important distinctions. One objection is that two doctrines, both of which *radically* assert the priority of the state (whether transitionally or permanently) over the individual are Communism and Fascism. According to our equation of collectivism with the "left", we have the immediate problem that within the same collectivist category, fascism is commonly called "right" and communism "left". How can we call both "left" (collectivist) and yet distinguish them?

The answer has to do with the locus of the substantive values chosen by Fascism and Communism. Fascism found its values in a mythical *past*. Its interest was in *restoration* of this abstraction (and in the case of highly traditional societies, this is in the maintenance of traditional folkways). Communism, on the other hand, found its values in a utopia of the *future*. Its interest was in the implementation of a *new* abstraction: in *revolution*. Nevertheless, both locate their ideal (notwithstanding the Marxist dream of the "withering away of the state") in a disciplined order of the state itself.[49] The difference is not in the preferred primacy of the state, but in the selection of the values of the state – historical or futuristic. We can therefore hold this modified concept of the "left" to describe both forms of statist doctrine. Indeed for the *individualist* (as for example, Karl Popper himself), the statism of Plato, Fascism and Communism are essentially three of a kind.

A similar objection arises in categorizing as "right" all doctrines which advocate the primacy of the individual over the state or ideals of collective organization. Amongst these are proponents of democratic, free-market, "small government" societies, who sometimes call themselves, and are called by others, "conservative". Equally amongst those who uphold the primacy of the individual, one finds extreme libertarian thinkers (not of the democratic socialist, but more of the "anarchist" or radical "existential"[50] kind). They could be said to be opposed to the existence of the state in virtually any form. In comparison with the "conservative" *laissez faire* capitalist or liberal pluralist, they have been called (far) "left" and beyond. Here, *within* the "individualist camp", the qualifying terms "left" (radical libertarian, anarchist, existentialist) and "right" ("conservative" *laissez faire*) hinge on the degree of structuredness and continuity of change to which they subscribe. The anarchist and radical existentialist are not bound to a concept of process in change. The conservative or liberal pluralist, on the other hand,

---

49 Cf E. Nolte in (L. Vennewitz [transl]) *Three Faces of Fascism: Action Française, Italian Fascism, National Socialism*, NY: Holt, Rinehart and Winston, 1965: "Fascism is an anti-Marxism which seeks to destroy the enemy by the evolvement of a radically opposed and yet related ideology and by the use of almost identical and yet typically modified methods, always, however, within the unyielding framework of national self-assertion and autonomy" pp. 20-21.
50 Such as found in the philosophy of Jean Paul Sartre, in the concept that "existence precedes essence".

will require structure and process in change. The anarchist and radical existentialist dispenses with both. This is a major polarity *within* what we have conceptualised as "right", and defies normal parlance which calls the anarchist and radical existentialist "leftist". Nevertheless for the statist, whom we have here classified as "left", both the anarchist and the liberal are subversive of the collectivist conception of the state. Accordingly, to identify a "right-left" with an "individualist-collectivist" dichotomy, the terms right and left must be distinguished from some of their common uses.

Our point here, however, is really not to wrestle all western thought into a right-left categorization, without further differentiation. It is sufficient to highlight the individualist and collectivist paradigms in the common examples of liberal democracy and social democracy which constitute the right-left political polarity found in many contemporary societies. These same *temperaments*, as we wish now to show, can find expression when committed to the framework of the specific values transmitted through the tradition of universal ethics from Sinai.

"Right" and "left" in universal ethics

In the history of general society, many movements of the right and left, were in fact at major variance with universal ethics. In the light of universal ethics, an acceptable position whether from the "right" or from the "left" must be consistent with those universal values. From the standpoint of universal ethics, there is an objective morality. It is wrong actively to kill a person under the rubric of "euthanasia"; "homosexual marriage" is similarly wrong. These have been prohibited by G-d, and do not constitute norms for which this world was created. Consequently, the expression of personal political temperament – "left" or "right" – cannot be *about* whether these norms should be implemented or not. If "right" or "left" involves a breach of universal values, then that "right" or "left" is an inadmissible expression of human personality and choice. Nor can "democracy" or any other political or judicial process authorize values which run contrary to universal ethics.

Thus, for example, the fact that a "democracy" has by its due process willed and enacted incestuous marriage (between half-siblings) in Sweden, does not make such a "norm" admissible. G-d mandated moral rules, not styles of political system or modalities of Government. Under universal ethics, for the "democrat" by temperament, "democracy" cannot validate all its possible decisions. The conjuring in it of a majority for immoral ends is no better than majority support for a totalitarian society with immoral policies. G-d did not allow that fundamental morality can be established or altered by mass opinions. Just as morality does not originate in the human mind, it is not alterable by a human mind, whether of one person or by a majority of persons. It may be the praise of grass-roots humanity that "you can't fool all of the people all of the time", as President Abraham Lincoln said, but it is possible, as he conceded, that "you may fool all of the people *some* of the time". Democracy is not a guarantor of morality, and therefore not an absolute in itself. It can, however, function worthily within the boundaries of universal ethics, that is to say, under G-d.

"Right" and "left" as a natural human diversity of temperament find legitimate expression where these express themselves *within* the parameters of universal ethics. For example, to give charity (to redistribute wealth in some measure) – or at the very least, not to be indifferent to the needy – is a requirement of universal ethics. But whether this shall be left to an unregulated private ethic of charity on the part of individuals (whether wealthy or not), or whether it shall be additionally accomplished by the state via taxation and welfare, are examples of "right" and "left" positions on charity itself, with a spectrum of positions in between.

So too, whether society will take upon itself *extra* strictures to safeguard social morality may also be a decision which finds difference of opinion between "right" and "left" positions within the framework of universal ethics. Thus, excessive gambling is a behaviour which on the micro- and eventually macro-scale is socially destructive behaviour. But shall the state intervene to require all gamblers on "poker machines" to undertake a "pre-commitment" of time and loss which will inhibit the gambler's losses? Or is this deemed an issue of individual self-control?

Not only *who* imposes the obligation, but more basically, what the *extent* of the obligation is, is relevant to the concepts of "right" and "left" in universal ethics. In fact, every major universal law, within basic parameters, admits of views of both minimalist ("right") to maximalist ("left") obligations in its performance. Thus, in the realm of economic behaviour, there are varying views about the extent to which one must protect and look out for the other (in benefaction), as distinct from simply not harming the other; there are varying views as to the degree of objectivity (stringency of proof of guilt) which a justice system must employ. The maximalist view does not take away from the minimalist requirements. It extends the minimum.

Whilst the extension of obligations ("maximalism") is often associated with the growth of the state and social administration, it need not necessarily be so. A wider degree of obligation to others and to one's Creator can also be internalised and self-administered by individuals. As noted, charity can be practised in a highly disciplined, quantified and committed way by individuals, through their own conscientious volition. A collectivist attitude can be implemented by individuals. Along the route to redemption *via* universal ethics, there can prevail both "right" and "left", individualist and collectivist, perspectives. Indeed, and this may be the ideal scenario, society will move towards a concept of *maximal* ethical obligation both towards our Creator and fellow humans, if and where possible through *individual* motivation and the fullest articulation of individual personality.

4
ETERNAL LAW AND HUMAN
LEGISLATION

In the concept-world of modernity, and its "flagship" movement, the "Enlightenment", little stands higher than the ideal of the autonomy of the human being. This movement sought to subject both authentic knowledge and morality to the human being alone. Ostensibly there is here a conflict between a Divinely revealed ethical norm and the very idea of human autonomy.

Such a challenge and its answer proceeds from different concepts of the human being. The standpoint of religious philosophy is that the human being possesses a spiritual affinity with the Divine and that in this dimension we find the *essential* human being. This may be expressed in terms of the human's soul being modelled upon the Divine, or the ability of reason to transcend private interests and participate in a Divine wisdom. The view which challenged this asserts the primacy of human intellect and material need and the will to their satisfaction. Here we look at two schools of ethico-legal theory in the general western tradition, which take up these positions: the teachings of "natural law" – eternal law – and "positive law" – human legislation. After that we ask, how the conflict between them – that is, between eternal principles and the registering and implementation of practical and personal interest or need – is resolved by the tradition of universal ethics from Sinai.

Conflicting paradigms of universal and human law

It is possible to argue for a classification of historical philosophies
of law in the western tradition into two broad categories exemplified
by "natural" and "positive law". The first, the notion of "natural
law", will include Greek and Roman law and medieval Christian
law, and finds its highest philosophical self-consciousness in the
writings of Augustine and Thomas Aquinas. In the words of A.P.
D'Entreves:

> ...the Roman doctrine of natural law...was borrowed
> wholesale from Greek philosophy... Mankind is a
> universal community or cosmopolis. Law is its expression.
> Being based upon the common nature of man, it is truly
> universal. Being endorsed by the sovereign Lordship of
> G-d, it is eternal and immutable. The doctrine passed...
> into the teaching of the Christian church... The lawyers
> of the Church... gave natural law an unprecedented
> coherence, clearness and force. Canon law has been said,
> and correctly, to constitute the principal vehicle, in the
> Middle Ages, of the doctrine of the law of nature.[51]

Natural law designates, according to Aquinas, a law which is *universal*
and *prior* to any particular individual or group of individuals who
seek to make law. It is *transcendent* in that it encompasses *all* humanity
and in that it forms a prior "rule and measure"[52] to use Aquinas'
words for the acceptance of any law. The "transcendence" of the
morality of natural law is also a transcendence of *time* and *place*
– the dimensions of particularity – and as such it is viewed as *eternal*
and *immutable*. The *immutability* of natural law, as eternal, prior and
universal is reconciled with the phenomenon of change in the
following terms:

> ...natural law is the same for all...the natural law is
> altogether unchangeable in its first principles. But in
> its secondary principles which...are certain detailed

---

51 *Natural Law – An Historical Study*, N.Y.: Harper and Row, 1965, pp. 20-21, 33.
52 *Summa Theologica*, XIII, Q. 90, ii.

proximate conclusions…it may be changed in some
particular cases of rare occurrence…[53]

F. Copleston explains it thus. Aquinas'

> …admission of the changeability of the secondary
> precepts of the natural law in particular cases refers
> rather to what the Scholastics called a *mutatio materiae*
> than to a change in the precept itself: it is rather that
> circumstances of the act are so changed that it no longer
> falls under the prohibition, than that the prohibition
> itself is changed.[54]

For Aquinas, there is, besides natural law, also a notion of human law
but "human law has the nature of law insofar as it partakes of right
reason; and it is clear that in this respect it is derived from eternal
law"[55]. That is, there is a concept of "human reason" in Aquinas but
this itself is subordinate to the natural law. The human reason which
is capable of attaining results consistent with natural law is, in the
words of Aquinas, something "instilled by G-d".[56] Human reason
contains within itself a *higher* reason, whereby it can discover the
natural, the Divinely enjoined law.

Natural law thus stands in opposition to the general second
category of law, "positive law", where the latter understood itself as
freely willed and humanly legislated law, as discussed below. Natural
law does not seek explanation or justification through any human
legislative activity; rather it is the transcendent standard of justice
which precedes and adjudicates the rightness of any law. In the oft-
quoted expression of Augustine: "It seems that a law which is not
just is no law at all".[57] The notion of natural law as the sole fount
and measure of valid law is expressed in the rhetorical question of
Augustine, "without justice what are Kingdoms but great bands of

---

53 *Ibid., XIII*, Q. 94, ii,iv,v.
54 Frederick Copleston, *A History of Philosophy*, Volume 2, part II, N.Y.: Doubleday (Image
Books), 1962, p.128.
55 *Summa Theologica* XIII, Q. 93, iii.
56 *Summa Theologica*, XIII, Q. 90, 1v; Q. 93, ii. .
57 *De Lib. Arb.* i, 5

robbers? What is a band of robbers but a little kingdom?"[58] It is religiously authenticated values which constitutes the standard for all governmental policy.[59]

The relationship of the results of natural law and its methodology to the universal ethics of the Noahide laws transmitted from Sinai are not our concern here; other than to note the view of a significant contemporary natural law theorist and Catholic thinker, Robert George, that

> The natural law is…a 'higher' law, albeit a law that is in principle accessible to human reason and not dependent on (though *entirely compatible with and, indeed, illumined by) Divine revelation*…Paul, for example, refers to a law 'written on [the heart]' which informs the consciences of…the Gentiles who do not have the revealed law of Moses to guide them.[60]

At all events, it is the clear view of natural law theory that if there is any concept of human autonomy, it is not one which provides "an autonomy of the natural reason for its 'own' norm-setting activity. The process of constituting the natural law by the natural reason is not a 'creative' process, but rather an unfolding of the participation of the eternal law in man."[61]

Positive law

In general secular legal theory, "positive law" is counterposed to the concept of "natural law". Just as natural law can be defined as a broad category, so also can positive law. The notion of positive law comprehends law as a human, political command. Insofar as it

---

58 *De Civit. Dei* 4,4.
59 Copleston, *op. cit.*, Volume 2, part I, p.104.
60 Robert P. George, "Natural Law, the Constitution and the Theory and Practice of Judicial Review", in Robert P George (ed) *Natural Law* Aldershot: Ashgate, 2003, p. 281 (Emphasis added).
61 M. Rhonheimer (transl. G Malsbary), *A Thomist View of Moral Autonomy*, NY: Fordham University Press, 2000, p. 286.

grasps law as socially or humanly originated, the characteristic of positive law extends to many post Renaissance theories of law. In this paradigm, law has to do with human will. Even the sociological or legal-realist jurisprudence of Roscoe Pound, which was concerned through law "to harmonize the satisfaction of wants"[62], falls in this category. It professes itself as the legal science of "efficacious social engineering"[63], but it is nevertheless concerned with *socially* perceived wants. Much modern legal theory sees the roots of law, not in a transcendent *beyond* but in the matrix of presently humanly and socially experienced need.

The Renaissance beginnings of the doctrine of the sovereign state, found in the writings of Jean Bodin, is the basis on which the theory of positive law could be developed. For Bodin the sovereign is the originator of law, the arbitrator of law and "a subjection of the sovereign to any kind of basic [i.e. natural or eternal] law would destroy the essential meaning of sovereignty".[64] It is interesting to note how sovereignty is comprehended in this essentially Renaissance mode as indivisible:

> ...[L]aw as positive statutory law must be clearly distinguished from any kind of law derived from morals and equity. This tearing apart of the two sides of law, which until then had always been considered intimately related and together constituting a unity, parallels in its historical impact the analogous separation of power politics and morals by Machiavelli. And although Bodin sharply rejects Machiavelli, it is undeniable that his precise argument in support of statutory law as the command of the sovereign is just as important a step in the direction of the modern state as that of Machiavelli.[65]

The Renaissance view of the sovereignty of the human vis-à-

---

62 *Op. cit.*, p.42
63 *Ibid.*, p. 47
64 C.J. Friedrich, *The Philosophy of Law in Historical Perspective* 2nd edn., Chicago: University of Chicago Press, 1963, p.58
65 *Ibid.*, p. 61.

vis the claimed universal authority of religious authority and its law finds its way into jurisprudence. Law making is focused in the person of the leader of the sovereign nation or city-state.

The novelty of the work of the Enlightenment figure and classical exponent of positive law doctrine, John Austin, is to connect law with *relationships* of authority. Austin states that law has the essential character of "command". That is, it is issued by one, whose law will be obeyed *by another*, since behind it lurks the possibility of punishment for its non-fulfilment. Law is promulgated by a *political superior*. The power of judges or customs becomes law only in that they are mandated by the supreme political body or individual. The concept of sovereignty thus carries with it a corollary of subjection. Its authority is not a Divine, but a human or political, authority.

Possibly, the most elaborate philosophy of law in terms of the relationships involved in sovereignty is to be found in Hegel's *Philosophy of Law*, where the State and particularly the Sovereign, the Monarch, is seen as the unification of the universal and the particular, the meeting of individual and collective goods. Marx's critique of Hegel's *Philosophy of Right*, is simply a critique of Hegel's *model*, and an intimation of his own version of the true, human constitution of the sovereign state. For both Hegel and Marx, law is law because of the human arrangements out of which it arises.

The underlying and common features of all the species of "positive" law which can be subsumed beneath the title "positive" is then that law originates in *human* – legislative, political, social and judicial – *activity*. Law is not *intrinsically* valid or imperative. It expresses human will, need and political power.

The rupture between ancient and modern secular law

In Henry Sumner Maine's *Ancient Law*, we find a profound characterization of the difference between the substantive qualities of ancient and modern law. We can argue that this difference

corresponds to the difference between natural and positive law, in
the broad senses of these words. Maine's famous distinction between
ancient and modern law, is summed up as the transition

> from one terminus of history…in which all the relations
> of persons are summed up in the relations of Family…
> towards a phase of social order in which all these
> relations arise from the free agreement of Individuals…
> a movement *from Status to Contract*.[66]

What this means is that ancient law reflects the traditional,
unchanging character of social relationships – i.e. *status* – such as
one finds in the structures of the family, the clan and so forth. This
can be seen in the laws of succession, where for example, the heir is
understood legally to represent the "posthumous existence" of the
one who bequeaths to him; where potential heirs are understood
virtually as partners in the estate which they will inevitably inherit. It
is understood in family law by the prescribed relationships of family
members[67]. So too in laws of property, we find that property is
conserved within families by laws of primogeniture and procedures
of co-proprietorship, which relates property to family or communal
groupings. In other words, law echoes and reinforces a normative
conception of what human relationships are held intrinsically to be,
in some "natural" or "organic" sense. Law enshrines status.

Modern law is different. It is the modern will (i.e. testament), on
the other hand, together with the legal institution of *contract*, which

> has exercised the greatest influence in transforming
> human society… Wills…become powerful instruments
> in modifying society through the stimulus they give to the
> circulation of property and the plasticity they produce in
> proprietary rights.[68]

In Hegel's philosophy of law we find how strikingly the institution
of contractually orderable proprietary rights is connected with the

---

66 *Op cit.*, pp.140-41.
67 *Ibid.*, p.140.
68 *Ibid.*, p.161-2.

notion of the sovereignty and freedom of the *human being* and of
the individual in particular. Hegel describes the freedom of the
human, as the ability to acquire things around one in nature, and
to deal with them as one pleases. Freedom is the ability freely to
dispose of property and this distinguishes the free individual within
modern society from an earlier society under a "natural" order of
humanity.

Consequently, the relations between people in a free civil society
are between themselves as owners of property, which can be 'brought
into parity, through being bought and sold' as 'subjects of contract'
and recognized 'objects of the will' [- of desire]".[69] The contractual
relationships of private property are the precondition of freedom.
Through them the human – the *individual* who breaks free from
all communal status bonds – can be what he or she wants to be,
away from what were regarded as the "frozen" social relationships
enshrined in an older law.

The substantive character of "ancient" (including medieval) and
modern law thus corresponds to the theoretical conceptions of
natural and positive law. Natural law expresses a conception of what
the human in a morally and existentially pre-ordained sense, *should
be*. This is the notion of *status*. Positive law facilitates through *contract*
what *the human wants to be,* and the law of contract is the perfection
of this instrument of free arrangement. Social relationships are
established by law through contract to satisfy needs; they do not
express any *intrinsic* values. Status, expressing unchanging laws and
values, becomes the polar opposite of a legal order of contract.
The legal order of contract can create relationships independent
of any pre-existing status. Contract is the universal instrument of
adjustment to arbitrarily chosen personal ends.

In summary, the conflict of natural law and positive law is that
natural law is concerned with values, which are held to be objective
values or goods in themselves. These are sometimes called "*non-*

---

69 Joachim Ritter, *Hegel and the French Revolution* transl. Richard Dien Winfield, Cambridge,
Mass.: M.I.T. Press, 1982, p. 137.

instrumental goods". Positive law understands itself as *instrumental* to particular human will (or harmonization of individual human wills on a social scale). It does not address abstract and intrinsically valid values but the autonomous exercise of human legislation. Typically positive law engineers *new* relationships between persons (and thereby ever new values) to achieve the ends of human will. Natural law *fuses* human autonomy, expressed in legislative activity, with the "natural" moral norm. Positive law, in the spirit of modern politics, *is able and ready to separate law from received moral norms.*

In reality, contemporary political systems contain mixtures of "natural law"– which seek to posit some fundamental enduring human rights and obligations – and "positive law", the free statutory power of the legislature. It could be argued that what is set out as "natural law", in some charters, is no more than recent positive law, seeking to enshrine itself for posterity. Others genuinely take over elements from tradition.

For the universal ethics in the tradition from Sinai, two questions remain: (1) where do we look for the enduring, intrinsically authentic *(non-instrumental)* values which law must enshrine? (2) alongside the legal and political incorporation of these values, what role is there for an "autonomous" legislative creativity which serves *(is instrumental to)* the fulfilment of the practical will and needs of human beings? Putting both questions together, how does the tradition from Sinai answer and accommodate the claims of both natural and positive law?

The "Written" and the "Oral" Law from Sinai

The "Written Law" from Sinai as revelation

The notion of a prior, given, transcendent law is expressed in the Biblical text, the Five Books of Moses, given to Moses at Sinai. The text of this law, known as the "Written Law", was revealed and received through "prophecy". It was received from G-d by Moses. The Five Books of Moses contain six hundred and thirteen commandments given to the Jewish people and seven commandments for humanity, the "Noahide laws".[70] The seven Noahide laws in fact contain very many derivative principles overlapping with much of the 613 laws given to the Jewish people. The composite character of this Revelation, as a set of laws for all humanity plus specific commandments for the Jewish people, has a symbolic representation in its essence, the Ten Commandments. Just as the full text of the Revelation, the Five Books of Moses, contain 620 commandments (Jewish and Noahide), so does the Hebrew text of the Ten Commandments, its core, correspondingly contain 620 letters.

The "Written Law", which is a Divinely *commanded* law, is an expression of the *Divine* Will, which transcends the "understanding" of created intellect. Whilst this Will is beyond reason *in its origin*, it can, however, subsequently *be grasped* (sometimes more and sometimes less) by reason. Having been given the law, we can proceed to attempt to understand it, and it is desirable that we do make this attempt. Nevertheless, it remains a *Divine* wisdom, and where reason falls short in grasping it, that does not diminish its authority. The reception of this wisdom or Law, was not through reason but through prophecy – ultimately a suprarational mode of access to a "metaphysical" realm[71] beyond human reason. Thus, the great medieval scholar, Moses Maimonides writes about the modality of prophecy:

> Prophecy is bestowed only upon a very wise sage of a strong character, who is never overcome by his natural inclinations in any regard. Instead, with his mind, he overcomes his natural inclinations at all times. He must

---

70 The biblical revelation at Sinai reiterates and gives conclusive authority and form to the pre-existing Noahide laws, which were already complete in the covenant made with Noah.

71 See Marvin Fox, *Interpreting Maimonides — Studies in Metaphysics and Moral Philosophy*, Chicago: University of Chicago Press, 1990, p. xi *et passim*.

[also] possess a very broad and accurate mental capacity. A person who is full of all these qualities and is physically sound [is fit for prophecy... [H]is mind should constantly be directed upward, bound beneath [G-d's] throne [of Glory, striving] to comprehend the holy and pure forms and gazing at the wisdom of the Holy One, blessed be He, in its entirety, [in its manifold manifestations] from the most elevated [spiritual] form until the navel of the earth, appreciating His greatness from them. [After these preparations,] the spirit of prophecy will immediately rest upon him.

When the spirit rests upon him, his soul becomes intermingled with the angels called *ishim*, and he will be transformed into a different person and will understand with a knowledge different from what it was previously. He will rise above the level of other wise men, as [the prophet, Samuel] told Saul [I Samuel 10:6]: "[The spirit of G-d will descend upon you] and you shall prophesy with them. And you will be transformed into a different person.[72]

Prophecy is not "cognition" but rather has a quality of spiritual "seeing". Moreover, in the tradition from Sinai, the validity of any prophecy depends on its consistency with the prophecy of Moses. And the "validation" of the prophecy of Moses in turn is based on the collective *prophetic* experience of the entire Jewish people, which stood and witnessed this prophecy to Moses at Sinai and passed it on to all future generations. Here Maimonides states:

What is the source of our belief in him [Moses]? The [revelation] at Mount Sinai. Our eyes saw, and not a stranger's. Our ears heard, and not another's. There was fire, thunder, and lightning. He entered the thick clouds; the voice spoke to him and we heard, "Moses, Moses, go tell them the following...[73]

---

72 *Hilchos Y'sodei HaTorah* 7:1 in the translation of E. Touger, *Maimonides Mishneh Torah, Hilchot Yesodei HaTorah - The Laws [which are] the Foundations of the Torah,* Jerusalem: Moznaim, 1989
73 *Hilchos Y'sodei HaTorah* 8:1 in E. Touger's translation of the *Mishneh Torah.*

Maimonides continues,

> ...if a prophet arises and attempts to dispute Moses'
> prophecy by performing great signs and wonders, we
> should not listen to him. We know with certainty that
> he [the new prophet] performed those signs through
> magic or sorcery. [This conclusion is reached] because
> the prophecy of Moses, our teacher, is not dependent on
> wonders, so that we could compare these wonders, one
> against the other. Rather we saw and heard with our own
> eyes and ears, as he did.[74]

In summary, the Written Law as revelation (delivered through
prophecy) as explained by Maimonides expresses an eternal,
transcendent, objective law prior to any constitutive human subject,
society or state. It *essentially* transcends reason. Any reasons which
can subsequently be adduced for it, true as they may be, are not
the *foundation* of its validity or acceptance. Thus, the tradition from
revelation does not "begin" with reason, but rather "ends" with it.
The texts of the Written Law are *revealed* texts which set out the
actual contours of Divinely mandated conduct.

The Oral Law from Sinai and human legislation

The "Oral Law" is the commentary on, and legislative elaboration
of, the Written Law. It was also given to Moses at Sinai and is called
the Oral Law because it was intended for oral transmission, not to
be written down. When through progressive elaboration, it became
too copious, and the generation too weak, to commit it to memory,
it was, by permission of the tradition itself, committed to writing.
According to Maimonides, the content of the Oral Law is threefold.
It contains laws given at Sinai (not intimated in the Biblical text,
but necessary for elaboration of the Biblical commandments).[75]
Secondly, it contains elucidations and detailing of the commandments

---

74 *Ibid.*, 8:3.
75 These are called *halachos l'Moshe miSinai* or *divrei kabbalah.*

for which there are often only cryptic allusions in the written Law. Thirdly, the Oral Law contains the various positive enactments[76], restrictions[77] and customs[78] which were *innovated* throughout the generations "to bolster the religion and to rectify society".[79] This third category is concerned not so much with interpretation as with innovation. It is the dimension of "human legislation" to be discussed here.

The six hundred and thirteen commandments given to the Jewish people and the seven general Noahide laws of the *Written Law* are *eternal*. It is prohibited either to add to, or to subtract from, them. On the other hand, we find humanly legislated laws being added in an ever growing multiplicity. This is true both in the Rabbinic tradition in the case of the Jewish law, and so also by properly constituted courts and legal authorities in the case of Noahide law. The accumulation of this human legislation does not violate the principle that the Written biblical law is unchangeable. Rather this human law works to bring the Written Law into worldly accommodation and application.

This expresses itself most patently in its enactments to *fortify*, or to find acceptable means to *lighten* the burden of, the fulfilment of the precepts of the tradition according to the specific needs of *time and place*. In this respect the purpose of human legislation within the tradition is to issue positive enactments which *increase* the observance of biblical precepts as well as *additional restrictions* in order to distance a person from *infringement* of biblical laws. So too, there are customs, which emerge or are innovated, serving to embellish and so to *endear* the performance of precepts. Human legislation may also facilitate a minimal performance, or even a way of acceptably avoiding or circumventing the circumstances which obligate one in a biblical precept, where its full performance would

---

76 *Takanos*
77 *G'zeiros*
78 *Minhagos*
79 Maimonides, *Hilchos Mamrim* 1:2

cause undue stress or have negative repercussions. The function of all this is to preserve the body of precepts of the eternal Written law by means of auxiliary legislation which registers the specific stresses and strengths of the historical moment.

Thus, in Noahide – universal – law, it is within the power of a court, in the spirit of the tradition, to add stringencies to protect fundamental ethical norms. For example, while the prohibition on incest in Noahide law may be limited to certain basic familial relationships, a society can extend this to further relatives. As a means of strengthening sexual morality in general, it may choose to take upon itself the stringency of pre-marital sexual chastity. Apart from restriction, it can for example, so require additional positive performances (or a more maximal interpretation of obligations) towards one's fellow, such as further duties of care and regard in the realm of damages not required by base-line law. It can raise or lower standards of proof (though not below a minimum set out in law) required for a legal conviction, corresponding to the level of social stability and law and order. Moreover, when it does introduce new requirements beyond the basics of the eternal law, it can back these up with the full sanctions of the law.[80] In all of these cases, the intent is not to alter the basic precepts but to preserve them through using acceptable leeways of stringency and relaxation in their performance. In all of this it is fulfilling an *instrumental role*. It is the "free" and creative human response to human need and human will, in order to "negotiate" and "navigate" the course of the Biblical law through particular social and human conditions.

This human law shares the characteristic of positive law in a specific sense. Positive law in the secular tradition, as noted, is ready to separate law from received moral norms. The above described human legislation in the tradition from Sinai is also distinct from the laws set out in the biblical text. Indeed, it is forbidden to assert that this legislation is part of the revealed written law. At the same time,

---

80 *Likkutei* Sichos, Vol. 5, p. 190.

there is an essential difference between positive law and human legislation in the tradition of universal ethics. Positive law could be, and often was, indifferent to received moral norms. The human legislation, however, which received its impetus, and travelled down alongside the transmission of the Written Law, from Sinai, was always concerned to *serve* the norms of the Written law.

Objective universal law and "autonomous" human legislation

What could be the meaning of human "autonomy" in the context of the tradition of universal ethics from Sinai? The souls of those who stood at Sinai ratified the manifestation of the Divine when they said "we shall do and we shall hear".[81] So too the voice of Sinai travels down to this day throughout civilization and finds the same ratification or resonance in the human *spiritual* consciousness (or unconsciousness) of humanity in every generation. The soul, made in the image of G-d, when exposed to the Divine and to the ethical order corresponding to the attributes of the Divine, *naturally* resonates with it.

A meaningful sense of human autonomy is therefore to be found in the human being as a *composite* of soul, mind and body[82]. The realm of freedom and autonomy opens up in the conflicts between these elements of the person and has to do with struggle which occurs in their midst. The concept of freedom borne of, and expressed, by this struggle, goes back to the Biblical sin of the "tree of knowledge". With that cosmic event, the spiritual lost its actual continuous sovereignty within the person. When physical desires and intellectual challenges were then able to drown out the voice of the soul, freedom was born. But it was born as the practical ability to do good or evil – to go with or against the imperatives of the

---

81 Exodus 24:7.
82 Much of the following draws on the work of Viktor Frankl. See S. D. Cowen, "Viktor Frankl: person, philosopher and therapist", *Journal of Judaism and Civilization*, Vol. 7 (2005).

soul. The soul did not and does not cease to be the highest faculty in the human being. Its moral knowledge is ultimate.

The proper exercise of freedom by the whole, composite person is to restore the sovereignty of the spiritual within the person; the objective is to align the mind and the body with the spiritual. But this is not a simple matter of domination of the psychophysical by the spiritual. The discord, the complaint and demands of the mind and the body must be heard and as we say today, "brought on board". In other words, whilst the soul is the guiding light of the person, it must yet listen to and answer the questions of the mind and the grievances of the body. The result is an application of the spiritual norm which "sits" with, and is then aided by, the intellect and emotions.

The materialistic concept of the human being and human autonomy, on the other hand, poses a conflict between human legislative freedom and a universal ethics based on Divine revelation. It removes the human soul as well as its nexus with G-d. It assumes that the essential human being is a physically and intellectually willing and wanting being, who in principle should be able to do *anything* (so long as, in the classic liberal version, this does not harm the comparable ability of another). To the extent to which it attenuates the spiritual in the human being and its role in society, the collision with a Divine norm becomes inexorable. Without a spiritual pilot, physical desires, material interests or personal dispositions (the new "first principles") acquire the advocacy of intellect, to produce a freewheeling human "autonomy".

Autonomy in human legislation in the tradition of universal ethics is given to human beings in order to register and reconcile conflict between these norms and the human being as an individual and member of society. Via its courts and government, operating in the spirit and knowledge of Noahide law (universal ethics) human legislation is given the power to determine when stringency and leniency, within the parameters of universal ethics, is appropriate. It can fashion buttresses for ethical social practice and, and as noted, give them the full sanction of law. It knows social strain and can move between the minimal and the maximal application of the ethical norm.

The "human" dimension has its own role here. In the previous chapter we saw how the humanness of individual personality can be expressed within universal law. Here, a second facet of humanness, namely "autonomy" as freedom and creativity, plays its role in the installation of universal ethics within the world. In giving the eternal law its human "fit", this autonomy expresses the essential partnership of humanity with G-d in the project to accommodate the Divine within creation.

PART 3.
CREATING A POLITICAL CULTURE
OF UNIVERSAL ETHICS

5
ENTRY POINTS TO A POLITICS OF UNIVERSAL ETHICS

The spiritual health of a society

The first point of entry to a political culture of universal ethics is an understanding of where ethics reside and where their condition may be "read" in a society, namely in the "spirituality" or "spiritual health of a society". The tradition of universal ethics, which comes from Sinai, is essentially a spiritual tradition. It has flowed into the spiritual consciousness of human beings, found resonance there and fashioned core beliefs which in turn motivate ethical conduct. The politician and legislator concerned with universal ethics must therefore first reflect on the spiritual state of society – upon its core beliefs and values. He or she must then, secondly, examine how proposed legislation may impact or re-educate (sometimes harmfully) core values. Finally, the politician must be concerned with how to nurture within society a spiritual literacy in universal ethics.

Core and symptom

Medicine speaks about cause and symptom. If a person is fundamentally healthy, then a mere symptom of ill health – a headache, a runny nose, a cough – could be treated with an aspirin, a spray or a lozenge purchased over the counter. A doctor would judge that because there is no deep underlying health problem, it is enough to *manage* the symptoms. If the symptoms become serious, or they indicate that something is systemically wrong, one has to look at the core health of the person, for an *inner* malady. Carrying the analogy to society, the inner health of society is the state of its values. The external symptom of ill health is socially dysfunctional behaviour. A healthy society can cope with individual dysfunctional behaviour by managing it through police, welfare agencies and so on. A society with rampant dysfunction and breakdown makes a serious mistake by seeking simply to manage the symptoms. It must examine its inner health, the values by which people actually live.

We see in our society increasing symptoms of violence, youths carrying knives, pursuing a spiralling drug-driven and alcohol-heightened life of crime. One answer is to increase police presence and to punish offenders more severely. Another is to find the root of the crime. The cause tends over and over again to be shattered families. The utterly false happiness of drugged or alcoholic bliss replaces the solidarity, security and warmth of a strong family life and the inner élan of self-transcending beliefs and principles. Our society participated in a global financial crisis driven by greed and indifference. It was successfully managed by Government stimulus spending. Has, however, the possibility of its recurrence been treated through inculcation of an ethic of social responsibility which reaches corporations particularly? There is a significant rate of teenage pregnancy and other "unwanted" pregnancy. The phenomenon of "unwanted pregnancy" was treated in Victoria in 2008 by one of the world's and history's most radical laws of abortion on demand. But it did not seek to address or redress, why these pregnancies occur or why they are "unwanted".

There are many features of social breakdown, which are not necessarily expressed through violence or aberrant outward behaviours. There can be a mood of depression, a culture of nihilism and despair, or simply a hollow hedonism, which does not yet come to violence or health breakdown. It has been said of Australian society some fifty to sixty years ago, that it "had a sense of family, social stability and optimism".[83] None of these are manifest today. But has political consciousness registered that anything is wrong at the core; and if so, that social policy needs to address it?

Contemporary politics and legislation have not been interested in the human core – in this case the distorted values, the damaged relationships – which have produced socially dysfunctional trends. Instead, it has worked only with the surface, the symptoms or behaviours themselves. This society saw the growth of indiscriminate abortion, and finally legislatively validated over wide areas abortion on demand. In so doing, it teaches the next generation of children that pre-nascent life is freely disposable. As for the promiscuity, or the lack of committed context, which produced those "unwanted children", there is no political agenda for action. Much of the media, and even the non-tabloid "intellectual" media, maintain their reader "interest" with explicit or subliminally sexual material. Nobody can escape the morally retrograde antics of the "celebrities" showcased on magazine covers at every supermarket checkout. No law and no legal consequence have taught anyone that sexuality should be associated with love, commitment and responsibility. As for the de facto couples culture, with its spectrum of non-commitment to professed commitment (though by definition unformalized), there is an agreed silence. But a Relationships Bill was passed to endow it with all the benefits of marriage and make it a vehicle for the functional equivalent of homosexual marriage.

The political scramble to service the trend, the desires – the symptoms – has produced social policy, which impacts upon and redraws the human core. It has taken up one of the impulses –

---

83 The comment cited is that of a former Australian Prime Minister John Howard in his biography, W. Errington and P. van Onselen, *John Winston Howard*, Melbourne: Melbourne University Press, 2007, p. 18.

homosexuality – with which, according to the Divine norm, the human being has been traditionally bidden to struggle. Through a host of laws, it was granted a normativeness equal to that of heterosexuality. Everyone will agree that the *general* program to eliminate bullying, is a worthy goal. Yet, on the pretext of eliminating bullying of homosexually inclined children, new Government sponsored programs were established in schools. They ask children, with as yet incompletely formed sexual identities, whether they would identify themselves as heterosexual or homosexual (with some other variations such as "bisexual"), or as yet "don't know". All those who nominate a homosexual identity, on the basis of present impulses, are then in effect "validated" or given "confirmation" as homosexuals. The result is to cultivate homosexuality in the fluid sexual identities of young teenage children. This redrawing of human nature into two opposite but equally normative (hetero- and homosexual) models, is followed by tacit redefinition of marriage, not in name, but in legislative fact through relationships legislation, which constructs the equivalent of homosexual marriage.

The redrawing of the institution of marriage is then followed by legislation which redraws the concept of what it is to be a child and parent, by allowing the "commissioning" of children through IVF and surrogate "mothers" for homosexual couples, single parents and persons to whom the child bears no biological relationship.

The society "turns on" gambling, giving it maximal prestige by making a Casino the centrepiece and emblem of a world city, Melbourne. It is then preoccupied with ways of limiting the social destruction caused by "problem gambling". It embarks upon a program to "metropolitanize" the city by making alcohol available through many new outlets including hairdressers and bookstores. Symptom management enters with programs for problem gambling and the familial havoc wrought by it; and extra police are brought in to cope with violence resulting from increased drinking. Its preoccupation with servicing the symptoms and its blindness or indifference to the cause in the state of the human core, has only compounded the illness at the core, which produces the symptom. Indeed Government has an utterly conflicted interest in the illness. From the 5.1 billion dollars spent by Victorians on gambling, the Government collects 1.6 billion in taxes.

Politics must now be concerned with the human centre, which involves reflecting upon, and affirming, the highest values which civilization has produced. It must return to basic relationships and institutions, such as the ideal of marriage and family. It must encourage the effort, commitment and self-giving which make relationships work and endure. It must value human life including pre-nascent human life. It needs to recognize that economic relationships are human relationships and cannot be governed by deception and greed. It must acknowledge the value of social stability, which means the abhorrence of violence and the cultures which promote it.

The life of the human spirit, which ongoing secularisation has made a matter of embarrassment, must be affirmed again. Arguably there is no greater succour, no greater inner resource a young (or old) person can possess than the strength of the spirit and the power of self-transcendence, self-control, responsibility and commitment to worthy altruistic ideals. The values ideal in our society has been helped into decline through the breakdown of the family, which was the major agency of the transmission of those values, and because recent generations have been deprived of a spiritual education. People who come from stable homes, which exemplified and transmitted traditional universal values are less likely to take drugs, to practice violence on the streets, steal, or treat with deceit those, with whom they are in contact. They are less likely to be wasteful of resources or cruel to animals, because they know these to be deliberate works of their Creator. They will be less prone to negativity and depression, they will embark upon and embrace a life worth living. Fidelity to core universal values must become the benchmark of social policy and legislation.

Spiritual literacy

As a working political ideology, contemporary secularist political philosophy – hedonistic materialism ("Hedonomat") – argues to silence or at least limit the role of a religious contribution to political discourse. The argument has two tenets. One is that religious arguments or religiously inspired values cannot be admitted because their foundation is an essentially "private" one found in personal religious experience. It cannot be publicly shared or communicated. The second is that religiously based arguments do not partake of critical rational analysis and evaluation. The two points come together thus: religion is not admissible to political discourse because it is outside "public reason".

The argument is flawed in both of its tenets. The argument that spirituality is private and not a "publicly" – intersubjectively – communicable experience is a secularist prejudice. Perhaps the most salient feature of human history is the phenomenon of religion, shared by great masses of peoples, not only as belief but in terms of the specific values which emerge from that belief. Moreover *amongst* the various traditional faiths we see a common acceptance of Divinely revealed values and a consensus on many of these values. This is an intersubjectively shared experience and understanding. It is a secularist prejudice or disability, that leads the group of strident secularists, *the minority of humanity*, who have no religious experience, to claim that religious experience is not public. This was expressed with an ostensible humility by important thinkers such as Max Weber (and after him Jürgen Habermas) who described themselves as "religiously unmusical" (i.e. "tone-deaf").[84] But that is ultimately no excuse. As much as the secularist is entitled to ask the religious person to use his or her reason, the religious person is entitled to ask the secularist to exercise and expose his or her soul. And if the latter cannot find one, then the secularist should be asked sincerely

---

84 J. Habermas and Cardinal J. Ratzinger (now Pope Benedict XVI), *Dialectics of Secularization*, San Francisco: Ignatius, 2005.

to ask whether one can perceive oneself (including one's intellect) as something finite, as the creature of an infinite Creator, Who is beyond all form, since He is the Creator of all forms. In brief, the exercise is whether this person can attempt and achieve self-transcendence.

The second tenet of the stance which wants to exclude a religiously based voice in politics is that the ethics which emerge from religious experience and *belief* are not rational and accordingly lack validity. This assumption is mistaken on *rational* grounds. Honest reason is compelled to recognize the fact that it works with certain first principles, which reason did not produce, but upon which reason rests and builds[85]. In the case of secularist philosophy, the most fundamental assumption – that the physical world is "all there is"– is itself an act of belief. It takes *something* – for example, *matter* – which the Creator has made, and makes it absolute (everything). What is really at issue here is not an opposition of reason and belief, but an opposition of beliefs. Reason(ing) can be erected upon the foundation of either of these basic beliefs: both can ride with the "ticket" of reason.

The shared root of the major religious traditions consciously supply a moral compass to most of humanity. About 70% of Australians, according to the last census associate themselves with traditional religion. Traditional religion acknowledges a Creator and the mirror of the Creator within the human being, namely, the "soul". Religion is not only about belief in a Creator and about providence and purpose in creation, traditionally called redemption. It has also to do with steady, objective transcendent values and these values derive from revelation. They were given by the Creator, not invented by humans. Religion is the source of explicit values which acknowledge revelation as their source. Paradoxically, it is the source, in secular humanist movements, of the concept of social justice, of charity. These values of religious origin are carried forth

---

85 *Likkutei Sichos*, Vol. 2, p. 561.

by secularist movements which now reject or forget the religious origins of these values. Yet for most of humanity, for whom religion is still a lived reality, the effective reason why one does not steal, is not a piece of social contract theory, but because it is *believed* to be wrong from an essentially religious context. The commandment not to steal is observed as a consequence of believing in the Creator, Who commanded it. The attitude of so many, that one should not steal only because one could be *caught*, is due to the attrition of a conscious sense of a Creator, in whose presence one is always standing. Religion, on the other hand, is internalised as practical conscience. It motivates to ethical conduct and, as has often been pointed out, is a tremendous resource for personal refinement and transformation.

As noted already, the separation of religion and state in the Australian and American constitutions was not intended to exclude religiously inspired values from the public square and from observance in public institutions. What it meant was that Government, from the top down, could not prescribe adherence to a particular religious sect, or require its officers to be of that religion. Religion, however, as a source of values within the public square, which can well up into social policy, is absolutely legitimate. To the contrary, to curtail the expression of religious values in public policy and institutions, which arise from public opinion and sentiment, would violate the separation of religion and state. It would install a religion of secularism, which purges religious values from social institutions and social policy.

Just as health policy recognizes the needs of the human body, and secular education recognizes the need for training of the mind, so also must there be an acknowledgment of the existence of the human soul and its "education". Each child is entitled to a developing understanding of personal religious outlook, in parallel with his or her own intellectual and emotional development. This is so particularly in an environment where family break-up impedes the transmission of religious values, beliefs and practices; and where also there is an information flood, much of it purveying questionable values, to which the individual adult and child is virtually indiscriminately exposed. There surely exists an entitlement to a spiritual literacy, and to an understanding of how personal religious outlook addresses the myriad challenges from the social, cultural and natural environment. Accordingly, it should be recommended through a bill of the Australian Parliament that the new proposed national educational curriculum contain at least an elective subject in religion through to matriculation level. This is a subject, which should have a broad enough template to allow different faith traditions to share a common space and to teach it in their own spiritual "languages". It should be taught by believers for those wanting to believe or grapple with belief. It should be quite distinct from those subjects which present religion through secular filters: the philosophy of religion, comparative religion, the history of religion or the sociology of religion; it should be religion itself, thought about and taught from the inside. It should be education in the spiritual, from within our shared religious heritage.

It may well be that proponents of atheism and secular ethics will also want to enter this space, as we have seen the latter trialed in NSW primary schools. A proposal for religious studies through to matriculation as an offering within a national curriculum need not be afraid of this challenge. Nor should it fear that it has opened the stage to the extremism and violence taught by certain groups claiming to speak on behalf of a great world religion. To the contrary: the template for this subject (allowing for certain differences of tradition) would have to be worked out together by proponents of the major world religions, with the goal also of affirming certain basic commonalities such as the coexistence of all human beings. The purpose after all is to articulate a *common* beneficent spiritual heritage, within which different cultural languages of that belief can find their own portion and nurture.

The potential culture of universal ethics

There is a profound *potential,* and entry point, for cultivating the "common spiritual heritage", and through it a political culture of universal ethics, in the predominant multi-cultural mix of national and international society: Judaism, Christianity and Islam. Indeed amongst the major eastern religions, Hinduism also shares this potential.[86]   The first point of focus is the substantive shared framework and values emerging from these world religions. This establishes an order of values of shared spiritual resonance and legitimacy clearly of practical value to a national society. From there we proceed to look at how cultivation of a potential global culture of these ethics, the Noahide laws in their biblical source, can contribute to the resolution of a major issue of international politics: the Arab-Israel conflict and its international repercussions in global terrorism.

Common ground of Judaism, Christianity and Islam

The secular adage, that the world religions are a source of conflict, if it has any hold in reality, is based only in perverted manifestations or appropriations of religion. In reality the great major faiths, Judaism, Christianity and Islam, which singly or compositely constitute most societies today have a fundamentally common moral and spiritual root. The task before us is to expose and present that shared framework, which is the basis for harmony, stability – and sanctity – in society. The elaboration of this common outlook is itself the foundation of the *political culture* which supports these ideals.

Judaism, Christianity and Islam are united, first of all, by the belief in one G-d, the Creator of all things. This belief in G-d is

---

86 As noted, the Biblical tradition states that Abraham, the great exponent of these laws, and common ancestor of the cultures of Judaism, Christianity and Islam, also sent "his sons to the East" (Genesis 25:1), they are also at the root of Hinduism. This also makes it possible to evoke resonance for these values in major Eastern religions. See S.D. Cowen, *Perspectives on the Noahide laws*, Melbourne: Institute for Judaism and Civilization, 2007. Our focus here is on Judaism, Christianity and Islam.

experienced by virtue of the fact that the human being possesses a soul, in terms of which the human being is called biblically "made in the image of G-d". The "image" of G-d in the human being is not any physical likeness, but has to do with the soul's "likeness" – its ability to recognize and resonate – with the Divine, with G-d and with G-dly qualities. This common spirituality constitutes the "grass roots" unity and the true foundation for the peace and harmony of all humanity. It recognizes one moral authority, G-d, and shares the values taught by G-d, Whom the human soul is capable of imitating. An American President John F. Kennedy once said that peace is established not through treaties and conventions, but in the hearts and minds of men (and women). It is the shared spirituality of humanity which alone can turn the hearts and minds of all humanity to peace based on shared universal values.

At this point it becomes crucial to distinguish the authentic expression of religion from its inauthentic expression. This is established through the stance of self-transcendence in the human being whereby the human soul is made manifest, and authentically recognizes its Creator. The essential standpoint of the believer is the knowledge that he or she is a creation of G-d, constantly sustained in existence by G-d. This must awaken a profound humility in the human being. What this means for the human being is that the soul – the "mirror" of G-d and the true servant of G-d – must have complete sovereignty within the human being. Private passion, private interest and private conceptions must not intrude upon the will of the soul to know G-d and to cleave to Him. Accordingly those who dress up political agendas, and particularly violent ones, with the name of religion are in fact appropriating a religious veneer to personal and particularist interests. To support or associate terrorism against innocents with the name of Islam would seem to be quite antithetical to the genuine submission to G-d and the desire to manifest G-dliness upon earth.

The three religions, whilst having their own cultures and customs, recognize a common source of ultimate values. All of these religions recognize the Ten Commandments given at Sinai to Moses. They are orthodox in the sense that they believe in a distinction between right and wrong, truth and falsehood. They believe that the criterion for right and truth is the Good which was communicated by G-d, and intended for His Creation. At Sinai through Moses a fundamental morality was reiterated, that was already known from the beginnings of humanity down to Noah and Abraham. Both Noah and Abraham kept seven fundamental laws, known as the Noahide laws. These laws are the *substantive* Abrahamic root of the world religions Judaism, Christianity and Islam.

The seven Noahide laws which were restated at Sinai have been reaffirmed throughout history down to the present in affirmations of the US Congress in 1991 and the Governor General of Australia, Major General Michael Jeffery, in 2008. They are: (1) the belief in G-d and rejection of its opposite, idolatry (2) reverence for G-d and the rejection of its opposite, blasphemy (3) sexual morality upholding the norm of the heterosexual union of man and woman and the rejection of adultery, incest and bestiality (4) the prohibition of theft with all its ramifications for a just economic order (5) the prohibition of killing, except in self-defence and where warranted for deterrence (6) a system of courts which practice impartial justice and (7) a rejection of unwarranted cruelty towards animals and upholding non-destructive use of the environment. These norms are not malleable, but eternal, constituting the shared moral compass of humanity. Further particular traditions and customs of the individual world religions do not detract from this shared moral common denominator.

The three religions share a concept of redemption. Redemption is a time of peace and harmony amongst humanity, a time when G-dliness will be manifest upon the earth. The true purpose of the human being through belief in G-d and moral conduct is to work towards the goal of redemption. Freedom was given to the human being not to rebel against a Divine order of values but rather to implement it. The proper use of freedom is the assertion of the spiritual within the person, the assertion of the soul over mere passion and mundane interest. Its end goal, however, is the transformation of the mundane and the fusion of passion with the goals of the spirit. It is this goal which drives repentance and self-transformation. Personal transformation leads then to the transformation of all creation and the manifestation of the Divine within creation.

The three religions all have a concept of a Messiah. It is here that differences appear as to the identity of the Messiah. A contemporary Christian thinker, Victor Styrsky, has wisely observed that, as far as the relations between the faiths is concerned, the identity of the Messiah is ultimately "G-d's business". The Messiah will be sent by G-d to complete the work of Redemption and to effect the sovereignty of the Divine upon earth. When he comes in truth – that is, when he achieves this – he will be recognised by all. Consequently, the individual conceptions of the world religions about identity of the Messiah should not obscure our common ground in the belief in, and aspiration towards, the Redemption, of which the Messiah will be the final agent. The three religions, however, hold that the quest for redemption must be the uppermost goal of the human being.

The world religions in a shared global political culture

Just as the world religions can discover a culture of common norms, and hence of peace within societies, so can they at a global level. It is significant that the greatest conflicts in the international realm – the Middle East conflict and the phenomenon of international terrorism – are conflicts between peoples of the world religions, but in essence not of the world religions themselves. To the contrary, the following discussion indicates that the biblical sources of the world religions themselves offer a framework for peace in the Israel-Arab conflict and that terrorism is in contradiction to this shared framework.

The secular political models or political cultures intended to support political peacemaking between Israel and its neighbours have broken down. What is called for now is a common political culture which is authentically rooted in biblical teaching. This is the ultimately shared ethics of the Noahide laws – G-d-given laws of civilized conduct for humanity – which resonate at a grass-roots level in the cultures of Judaism, Christianity and Islam.

The land of Israel was given by G-d to the Jewish people as a Jewish land. It is the only land in which Jews can eventually perform the specific commandments given to them at Sinai in their entirety and this is its special sanctity. No "democracy" can will this away. It was recognized even by the not particularly religious founders of the Israeli State, who acknowledged the special place of Judaism in the State. This spiritual characteristic relates to the entirety of the land of Israel according to its Biblical boundaries. At the same time, the tradition from Sinai always acknowledged the possibility and conditions of the coexistence of Jews and non-Jews within the land of Israel. Verses in the Bible prohibit idolaters[87] from dwelling within the land. Nevertheless a non-Jew could live in the land by acquiring the status of a *Ger Toshav* – a "resident stranger" – through acceptance in a Jewish court of the Noahide laws together with the basis of their legitimacy, the revelation at Sinai. Not only may a *Ger Toshav* dwell in the land. He or she is also entitled to receive care and welfare from the Jewish people, like a Jew. Whilst the procedure for acceptance of a *Ger Toshav* does not exist presently[88], nevertheless major authorities of the tradition have stated that an equivalent for it exists – whereby a non-Jew may live within the land and be entitled to its welfare, like the *Ger Toshav*. The procedure to attain this status is the verbal affirmation of the Noahide laws (and their source in the revelation at Sinai). This status, however, would be an enduring residency in the land, not a political empowerment to overturn the

---

87 Signifying not simply idolatry but all forms of barbarous behaviour.
88 It obtains at a time when the Jubilee year is practiced.

Jewish character of the land. Just as the *Ger Toshav* was not permitted to dwell on the borders of Israel, so as to open up a security risk to the land, so too the non-Jews in the land of Israel cannot be allowed to jeopardize in any way the nation's physical security. In addition, the extent to which they maintain a level of civilized conduct of the Noahide laws, determines the extent they may be self-governing and autonomous. To achieve this, the resident populations must therefore be detached from the essentially secular politics of Hamas and other entities hostile to Israel – which merely adduce Islam as a religious veneer of legitimacy for their particularist politics. By the same token the proposal to make them take an oath of political loyalty to the Israeli state may also be mistaken. It imposes a secular politics, when the real allegiance is to be found in the common religious culture of the Noahide laws, which already acknowledges Sinai and resonates with the traditions of Islam and Christianity themselves.

Just as the Noahide laws provide the ultimate cultural-spiritual foundation for peace within the land of Israel, so also it is necessary to encourage a global culture of the Noahide laws. The very same conflicts being played out in Israel, and between it and its neighbours, are taking place now between world cultures. On the international scale, there must be cultivation in Christian and Islamic cultures of the common ethic and spirituality of the Noahide laws. The terrorism which dresses itself up in a veneer of Islam, is in absolute contradiction to the Noahide common denominator. The moral relativism which appears in the governments of Western, Christian society, in Europe and of late in America, unhinges them from the Noahide origins of their culture. Only the sense of a common spiritual authority and a common substantive ethics (including laws prohibiting theft and murder) can fashion the political culture of a cohesive international *society*.

Forging a political culture of universal values

After looking at the spiritual location and the cultural potential in contemporary society for a politics of universal ethics, it remains to look at the conditions of its actualisation. This final section, based on a forum held with Victorian state politicians, considers the relationship between a grass roots culture of universal values and politics; how faith groups must be inwardly and outwardly aggregated into a conscious and articulate culture of universal ethics and how politics must be exposed to that culture; and finally how the individual politician informed of universal values must have the *courage* to pursue these values in the political realm.

The informing of individual politicians

In the legislative year of 2008 in the Parliament of the Australian state of Victoria, values overturning those of the traditional faiths were socially implemented by Acts of Parliament: abortion law reform, relationships legislation and assisted reproductive treatment were all included in that year's legislation and have been discussed in an earlier chapter. For the most part, they were passed as a result of "conscience votes", in which individual parliamentarians could vote freely, not bound by party discipline. Reserved as "conscience votes", none of these issues (with the exception of the Relationships Bill on which the Labor Party did not allow a conscience vote) featured in the policy platforms of either of the major political parties.[89] That is, at the time neither major party was *entirely* a coherent vehicle for the key traditional values of civilization, which were challenged by the legislation. The question accordingly arises of how a political culture of basic, universal values can be created and find political vehicles for its implementation in all the major parties. This issue was

---

89 The Greens unequivocally embraced these changes whilst the two major parties were internally divided on these issues. In the traditionally "left of centre" Labor party most rank and file voted overall for the above bills; whilst most rank and file of the coalition of the traditionally "right of centre" Liberal and National parties voted against them.

addressed by three Victorian State Liberal politicians (subsequently elected to Government), themselves believers in fundamental values of the tradition, at a forum held by the Institute for Judaism and Civilization on 18 October 2010. The following is a summary of their contributions to this general question with interpolated commentary.

One of the questions which concerned members of the faith groups at the forum was why such basic issues as those mentioned (the life issue of abortion in the Abortion Law Reform Act and the question of the normative familial unit and homosexuality in the Relationships Act and the Assisted Reproductive Treatment Act) were avoided by the major parties in their platforms.[90]

A member of the forum, Robert Clark, subsequently re-elected to serve as Attorney General, had personally voted in the conscience votes for traditional values, notably against the bill enabling abortion on demand, a piece of legislation which he termed "very sad and retrograde". He was asked what would be the prospect of a change in any of this legislation were the Liberal-National coalition elected. His answer was that this would depend on the individual composition of the Liberal party and its choices in a future conscience vote: but that these issues would not become party policy. He explained that the American system, with an independently elected President, could allow candidates of the same party to campaign on more individualistic platforms. On the other hand, in the Australian (Westminster) system of "responsible" Government, which makes the Government's existence and stability dependent on its support by a majority of the Parliament, a stronger party discipline is required. To maintain party unity, certain areas of significant differences of opinion amongst party members, had therefore to be relegated to a conscience or "free" vote. Were they not, it would most probably

---

90 In party platforms these have been replaced with a jockeying for the political centre over managerial and logistical questions (water supply, law and order, jobs) all of which were important but were fundamentally consensus issues, which have to do with competence, not values.

drive out of the party many who would otherwise stay in on the agreed common policy. He chose to belong to the Liberal party, and personally to argue vigorously for the (faith-based) values in which he believed.

Whilst this answer could be understood, what solace did it offer for those who believe that the most fundamental moral issues must find strong and consolidated representation in politics and be brought to the electorate as party policy in an election? The conscience vote is typically held mid-term, far from elections, divested of party responsibility and accountability to the electorate. Mr Clark addressed the question by explaining that politicians could be made accountable to the electorate on the stand they took in conscience votes. He cited the words of Edmund Burke, that while politicians are elected to exercise their judgment, they will have to account for it at the next election. Indeed, after this forum, in the subsequent 2010 election, a Pro-Life group effectively campaigned against those individual candidates in marginal electorates who in the conscience vote of 2008 had voted for the legislation providing abortion on demand.

Robert Clark's point is that ultimately political culture, and the changes which occur within it, will affect politicians both individually and collectively as parties. Eventually, he stated, politicians are going to reflect the views of their electorate. This is why faith communities must hold public forums and directly engage with, and present their views to, politicians. Politics is made *in the public arena*, and ultimately the parties, whether collectively or individually in their membership will register changes in public opinion.

The aggregation of faith communities and forcing political issues into the public realm

Another participant in the forum, Mrs Inga Peulich (then Shadow Parliamentary Secretary for Education and Communities), had worked effectively to defeat a euthanasia bill in the Victorian Parliament. She voted against the Abortion and Relationships and Assisted Reproductive Treatment bills. She stated the moral principles which had guided her votes. Abortion on demand[91] was a clear negation of the rights of an unborn child. She argued that the existing "Victorian Charter of Human Rights and Responsibilities", itself a piece of the Labor Government's legislation, facilitated it by excluding rights of the unborn child. Euthanasia is "state sanctioned death", wrong in itself for the sick and aged, for whom palliative care is required. She described a legalized euthanasia as dangerously extendable to children, depressed individuals and plain "accidents" such as the 1000 involuntarily euthanased individuals in the first year of the Dutch legalization of euthanasia. On the issue of assisted reproductive legislation, she has written that the rights of the child must be the paramount consideration, which include, as part of basic identity, the right to a mother and father (something taken away by the Assisted Reproductive Treatment Act of 2008). The rights of the child had been omitted from the Victorian Charter of Rights and Responsibilities, passed by the then Government, and had been systematically violated by much legislation.

Mrs Peulich made a point to the faith groups themselves. There is a great need for the faith groups to articulate their own value positions and to make them fully known to their *own* constituents, many of whom are ignorant of them (in other words: spiritual literacy must begin within the faith publics themselves). Then there is a need for religious groups, sharing these fundamental values to aggregate their voice. Jewish, Christian and Muslim (and for that matter other, such as Hindu) groups are all part of this potential coalition. The faith communities have to appreciate clearly the practical importance of their alliance with one another, which is practically maintained by a sensitivity to differences. Community faith-based schools need to be

---

91 In the legislation, up to 24 weeks gestation without any questions, and up to nine months gestation on the basis of two opinions, the second of which did not have to be a medical opinion.

strengthened. Together, the faith groups must rise to the challenge in an environment where their values are threatened by rivals which are "better organized, better funded – sometimes by Government agencies themselves".

She stated also that the only way to preserve shared values of the world traditions is to make sure that all debates are brought out into the open. This was her method in leading the defeat of the Euthanasia bill: to force public hearings.

One could add to this statement, that only when the voice of the human spirit – the human soul and the eternal Divine values which it mirrors – is *heard* in the public sphere, will it receive its proper resonance, which even the libertarian media will acknowledge and follow, not wanting to be too far "out of step" with the real news and trends. Against this operates a covert political strategy, which seeks to prosecute religious views on homosexual practice as "hate speech" and to staff Government commissions or agencies with personnel committed to its ideological ends. It is insulated from public accountability, sealed away from grass roots and native human spirituality. Intellectual elites possess an occupational hazard of *hubris*: aware of their own intellectual powers, and absorbed with their expert "scientific" command of things, they face the *test* of forgetting their Creator and their own creatureliness. Not so the straightforward "grass-roots" public. This is not a statement of anti-intellectualism: rather it calls for the marriage of intellect with humility – the humility which steers intellect towards the source of universal ethics. Such use of intellect becomes a genuine guide for the "grass-roots" public.

Political courage

David Southwick, the endorsed Liberal candidate (and subsequently elected Member) for the electorate of Caulfield was the third politician in the forum. He frankly embraced the notion of restoring community based on traditional values and especially with regard to the young. He viewed society as being in danger of losing the moral compass represented by the shared root values of the world faith traditions, found in the Noahide laws. He observed that there had been harm done to education in these values, something traditionally cared for also by the family; harm done also to community and to the internal communication – "conversation" or "connectivity" – within community. Southwick stated that children need to be brought back to "belief", in a sense of what is right and wrong, and nourished in an optimism for life itself ("It disturbs me when I hear children talking about suicide"). The fundamentals which have been with us for centuries, the core moral "reason for which we exist" must be retrieved in education and community so that children can live happily and healthily into the future.

Elaboration of this point by David Southwick brings one back to one of the deepest requirements of education, the opportunity for children to expand their spiritual literacy. The birthright of humanity includes recognition and development of one's spiritual faculties as much as any other physical or intellectual actualisation. It needs to be offered in as vigorous and engaging a way as any other literacy or skill set. Children will never be able to preserve their heritage of faith, if they are not educated in it with a sophistication and vitality which matches their secular education, to deal with the inputs and blandishments of the secular culture, pouring into minds of children through modern media.

David Southwick extends the value set, to which society must be returned, also to value stances curbing the excesses of corrosive social trends. Gambling and drinking has opened itself to wide commercial and government exploitation and abuses. As noted, Victorians spend 5.1 billion dollars annually on gambling and the Government takes from this 1.6 billion dollars in taxes. There is consequently a Government interest in, and a Government accountability for, gambling and its impact on society. These issues must be addressed through education but also legislatively. He stated that, once elected, he would seek to deal with these through legislation in a balanced and sensible way. Business should be encouraged, but it should also be directed to ways which do not exploit children such as with mobile phone debt; they must be educated to a personal financial literacy and an ethic of personal responsibility.

With regard to the values of the moral compass, which were lost during the last Parliament, he committed himself to action. He stated that he would do what he could to reopen the discussion on abortion. He would look at reverting to the law as it stood with the "Menhennitt ruling", under which abortion could be justified when there was danger to the mother and not become a regime of abortion on demand. To this one could add that a culture needs to be cultivated, which replaces promiscuity and an ethic of irresponsibility with a sense of commitment in relationships and of the value of life.

The moral and hope of such a stance is that a single, articulate, strong voice can penetrate and crack a wall of political correctness. And it does not ultimately matter who says it. No human is perfect, we are not trapped in our past. A politician who has had an abortion can now genuinely believe and say that abortion on demand is wrong. We are capable individually and collectively of restoring our orientation to the traditional compass of the human spirit, the human soul. The time has come to add courage to conscience.

Lightning Source UK Ltd.
Milton Keynes UK
UKHW011112290719

347015UK00004B/1332/P